What Do Men Want?

What Do Men Want?

Masculinity and Its Discontents

NINA POWER

ALLEN LANE
an imprint of
PENGUIN BOOKS

ALLEN LANE

UK | USA | Canada | Ireland | Australia
India | New Zealand | South Africa

Allen Lane is part of the Penguin Random House group of companies
whose addresses can be found at global.penguinrandomhouse.com.

First published in Great Britain by Allen Lane 2022

002

Copyright © Nina Power, 2022

The moral right of the author has been asserted

Set in 12/14.75 pt Bembo Book MT Std
Typeset by Jouve (UK), Milton Keynes
Printed and bound in Great Britain by Clays Ltd, Elcograf S.p.A.

The authorized representative in the EEA is Penguin Random House Ireland,
Morrison Chambers, 32 Nassau Street, Dublin D02 YH68

A CIP catalogue record for this book is available from the British Library

ISBN: 978-0-241-35650-0

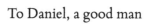

To Daniel, a good man

Contents

Introduction

Men and women exist. Occasionally, we even like each other.

We exist because of these two simple truths. We all owe our lives to the fact that it is possible – at least sometimes – for men and women to get along. All human life stems from the reality of, and difference between, men and women.

We live, however, in an age which is increasingly keen to pretend that sexual difference isn't important. In some respects, it isn't. The past century has seen women's mass entry into politics, culture and the labour market under the banner of equality. Men and women are becoming closer in terms of what they do, or want to do, and this has, in many ways, created a more complex and interesting world. The sexes are socially, economically, educationally, culturally and sexually more proximate in their behaviours than ever, and yet, in other ways, men and women could not seem further apart or less comprehending of each other. Chaos reigns.

The modern individual is, in many ways, a neutral, desexed being. The differences between us are papered over – in most contemporary workplaces it doesn't matter if a man or a woman does the job (although men still dominate the most perilous occupations), and it doesn't matter if a consumer is male or female, except if you are trying to sell them something branded, usually unnecessarily, as masculine or feminine.

We live at once paradoxically in a sexualized culture, and a world that would like to forget about sex. Playful androgyny, a kind of knowing messing about with roles, while not denying the reality of sexual difference, belongs to a distant era – think

of stars from the 70s and 80s: Bowie, Prince, Grace Jones, Marc
Almond, Boy George, Annie Lennox, and others. The popularity of drag indicates that there is great interest in the exaggerated
stereotypical performance of femininity (and to a lesser degree,
masculinity), but the undecidability of androgyny is a more
delicate proposition, one which we seem to have lost in the bid
to give everything a fixed name and an identity.

I think we need to return to thinking about men and women
in terms of 'sex' rather than 'gender', where the latter is a stand-
in for how people would like to be perceived by others. It's not
that how we would like to be seen doesn't matter, though it is
all-too-compatible with a culture obsessed with branding, but
that by ignoring sex we end up ignoring fundamental aspects of
our shared reality, and remain mired in confusion about who we
are and how we should understand each other.

Human beings always seem to live in one state of confusion,
crisis or chaos, or another, but lately our collective relation to
biological reality appears to have been shattered completely in
favour of something else, a 'gender identity', that is to say, an
inner feeling that one is a man, a woman, neither, both, sometimes one and sometimes the other, or something else entirely.
And that this identity need not bear any relation to biological
sex whatsoever. This is what Kathleen Stock identifies in *Material Girls*, as 'the trend in favour of gender identity and away
from sex', noting that 'a generational divide has opened up'.[1]
The battle of the sexes has become the battle *over* the sexes, and
anyone cleaving to 'essentialism' or to biology, that is to say
upholding the commitment to the reality of sexual difference as
fundamentally constitutive of all human life, runs the risk of
being threatened with violence, or losing friends and work as
various campaigns gear up to punish women (in particular, but
not only) for defending their sex-based rights.

As one article about Stock has noted, 'As one of the UK's

leading gender-critical feminists, who has insisted that an individual cannot change their biological sex, Professor Stock has faced relentless criticism and abuse . . . with blogs, petitions and Twitter users regularly demanding her dismissal for her allegedly "transphobic" views.'[2] Stock is not alone. J. K. Rowling received violent threats after she defended Maya Forstater, a tax specialist who had her employment contract pulled after being accused of posting 'transphobic' tweets. Forstater, having lost her initial employment tribunal, won on appeal in June 2021, with the judge stating that the belief that biological sex is real, immutable, important and not to be conflated with gender identity, is protected by law. Many other women, including myself, have had talks and shows cancelled, have been harassed and defamed for suggesting that women's concerns need to be taken seriously in the face of proposed legal changes to the meaning of the words 'men' and 'women'. Optimistically, one hopes that these kinds of campaigns to ruin people – which more and more citizens and employers are becoming aware of, and are often described as 'cancel culture' – will have their day. That institutions will stand up for those they employ, and that, where there is a clash of rights, people will sit down together and work out the best solution for everyone. At the same time as *this* battle over sex has been happening, another war is being waged. This one is against men, the whole damn lot of them!

To take just one recent example, in 2020's *I Hate Men*, French writer Pauline Harmange states that men are 'violent, selfish, lazy and cowardly . . . men beat, rape and murder us.'[3] When men complain that they have been unjustly maligned and generalized against, Harmange has little sympathy: 'All that time they spend snivelling about how hard it is to be a poor persecuted man nowadays is just a way of adroitly shirking their responsibility to make themselves a little less the pure products of the patriarchy.'[4] Men today are a legitimate target for hatred. Historically, we might say 'about time!' and this indeed is where we are at, although we should note that men were actually declared 'over' a while ago. In a 2010 article, Hanna Rosin asked, 'What if the modern, post-industrial economy is simply more congenial to women than to men?'[5] If more than a decade ago, Rosin could pose such a question at the level of the economy, today the question of men is posed at the level of culture. Men have had it too good for too long, the cry goes up. They are responsible for the vast majority of violence. They act like they deserve good things to come to them. *Their days are numbered.*

In 2009, I wrote a short, polemical book, *One-Dimensional Woman*, about women's place in the world as I saw it then. The text focused on the ways in which women were increasingly encouraged to participate in the labour market, how they were encouraged to identify as 'workers', and how they were depicted in contemporary culture. It didn't have too much to say about men, but nor did it especially denigrate them.[6] What I saw facing women in the 2000s was not blunt misogyny, but rather the opportunism of a culture that sought to 'sell' feminism to women, and, against the backdrop of the closure of largely male-dominated industries, how workplaces were increasingly branded as 'female'. Men and women were, as so often, being pitted against one another in the name of someone else making a profit. I think that we have moved to a new phase in this divisive process, one that plays out less at the level of work and the economy, but more at the level of how we interact. This runs alongside the decline in the interest of class as a category in favour of privileging identity. It is no longer our relation to the means of production that matters – whether we are exploited for our labour – but rather how we identify, and whether our identity is a good one (and therefore uncriticizable) or a bad one (therefore open to being blamed). Men as a class today most definitely fall in the latter category.

There are, of course, a *small number* of men who behave as if the world, and the women in it, owe them something. Of this there should be no doubt. Some men are extremely violent. Some men are in power. *These men, however, are not most men.* In my experience, and statistically, the vast majority of men are kind, thoughtful, self-aware, interested, compassionate, loving and protective, as friends or as partners. Perhaps I have been lucky. Yet, I don't think so. Many women would, I think, say the same thing. Most men are, like most women, a mixture of good and bad, but they are not, as a rule, irredeemable.

Bashing men is also *easy*. It is much more difficult, but ultimately much more worthwhile and, I would suggest, necessary, to wonder how we might live together better, about how men and women might be reconciled to one another's existence. If we all want to live better together, there needs to be much more constructive thought about how we do this. Is it useful to attack one class of people? Would this have the effect that we want, namely to get men to stop behaving in ways we don't like? What if it in fact has the *opposite* effect, and pushes men further into the arms of ideas that are hateful towards women? Wouldn't this increase the likelihood of resentful, and potentially violent, behaviour? Collectively, we all more or less want the same thing: to live together in harmony, to minimize harm, to get help for people in trouble, to acknowledge hurt, and to receive justice. People disagree on the means to achieve these ends. Some call for an increase in the prosecution and punishment of men who commit crimes against women. This might indeed serve as a warning to other men, and reduce such harm. Some want to dismantle this nebulous thing called 'patriarchy' altogether. I increasingly think that we need to think less in terms of structures (and patriarchy would be one such structure), and much more in terms of mutual respect. About how we get along day-to-day rather than in terms of vast, oppressive systems, whose image only makes us all more powerless. Men and women *are* different, but we have forgotten how, and there are always new ways of understanding these differences, but neglecting them altogether reveals the absence of a common understanding of who we are, as a whole.

One of the problems of today's dominant and negative way of talking about men in terms of their 'power' and 'privilege', is that it paints these attributes as *essential* features, as if men are just born with these things, and that there is little to be done about it other than complain. The idea here is that men largely treat women with contempt, or would do if they could only get away with it more. But if men are just 'like that', if they somehow constitutively loathe and disrespect women, then how can anyone do anything about it?

Let's start with some important questions: Are most men really misogynist? I don't think so. From the standpoint of spending time with women and having and looking after children, it wouldn't make sense for them to be so, unless something has gone terribly wrong with the culture in general. No doubt a small number of men (and a few women) *do* resent 'all' women and detest 'all' men, respectively, but these are unusual and extreme positions. What we encounter instead in our daily lives, in ourselves, is a vague mix of different thoughts and feelings that circulate in an inconclusive way. We do not always know how we feel about somebody as an individual and how we think about them in relation to their sex. The connection between someone as a 'person' and someone as a 'man' or a 'woman' is surprisingly ambiguous: we might judge someone we meet for the first time on the basis of their interests, appearance, manner, and so on, but we also see sex, however tangentially. So we encounter each other as people and as 'man' or 'woman' (or perhaps, occasionally, 'not obviously either') simultaneously. We probably all have prejudices one way or another about the opposite sex, but we are also surely capable of seeing people for who they are, beyond, but not completely without, the sex that they are.

If we want to live together in a healthier way, however, we must be committed to the idea that transformation is possible, and that people can become better human beings, capable of overcoming difficult situations and refining their beliefs. Otherwise, we will grow increasingly apart and segregated, not only by class and country, but by race and sex. There may be, of necessity, times when men and women *want* to be apart, or have spaces to themselves, but if we are committed to a mixed world, then we must be truly committed to it, to not shy away from who we are, in all of our positive and negative aspects. Our post-Christian age is extraordinarily unforgiving, often tying people to a single mistake they've made, or treating people as mere examples of a negative category, rather than as complex individuals in their own right. As many celebrities have learned to their cost, but ordinary people too, the internet never forgets. If you tweeted the 'wrong' thing at a certain point, said something clumsy or deemed to be 'harmful', or if you once upset someone, you will always have people on hand, usually people you've never met, to remind everyone of your 'sin'.

Currently, just as women have been in the past (that witch made my field barren!), men are often blamed as a whole for the actions of a few. But a punitive logic that sees no possibility of change helps nothing. Instead, it seems designed, perversely, to keep things exactly as they are, in a kind of stalemate of the sexes. Our culture often seems to combine the promotion of and prurient interest in hedonistic behaviour alongside a puritanical morality – we live in a *pruritanical* world, we could say. In other words, on the one hand, we are encouraged to have fun, to be completely selfish and pleasure-seeking, but, on the other, if we make a mistake, or become the target of others, there is no limit to the social punishment that can be meted out.

What is often forgotten today is the possibility of forgiveness – for oneself and for others. Without forgiveness, and the acceptance that we all make mistakes sometimes, we are all doomed to suspicious isolation. To understand the opposite sex, though, we must first perhaps understand ourselves. As psychoanalyst Massimo Recalcati puts it in *In Praise of Forgiveness*:

> The work of forgiveness, when it is successful, breaks the constitutive relationship between the I and the paranoid-narcissistic violence that drives it. It is a reversing, a withdrawal, most importantly a redesigning of one's own image . . . The work of forgiveness is first and foremost an extreme reckoning with one's own ideal image, to the point of understanding its real limit.[7]

All of which is to say, simply, that before we reach to blame those on the outside for our misery, we might first have to come to terms with our own expectations. It seems clear we are undergoing a sea-change in social mores. It may be that things that were acceptable and even playful or ambiguous a few years ago are now no longer permitted, even if these behaviours are not yet illegal (perhaps non-regulated flirting will become illicit in the future, for example). So, what kind of world do we want to live in together?

Let's try to be honest. As I've said, the vast majority of men I've met have been good to wonderful. I love my father, who has been a fantastic role model in every respect. My brother, too, is a kind and funny husband to his wife and attentive dad to his son. I love and have loved a small number of men a great deal, and I've been friends with some men for many years. I've had a few long-term relationships with men, and I adore these men still. A couple of men have behaved, at times, in ways that have hurt me, and some relationships I've had in the past have been less than ideal. I've caused pain too, for which I accept blame. I've been close to men who've committed suicide, which leaves something that feels like bullet holes in the soul. The vast majority of men I encounter in everyday life are interesting and interested, and even the ones I don't get along with I often admire for something in their way of being. All of this, I am sure, is not an unusual range of experiences for any woman who likes men, and who enjoys spending time with them.

It seems strange to say this, but being an adult involves taking risks, with one's heart, with one's trust, and sometimes with one's well-being. Despite the dominant idea that we should do everything we can to protect ourselves from potentially negative outcomes, life is dangerous. It's just not possible to always know what to expect, for better and worse. As adults, we have to come to understand that to live – to truly exist, to love – carries with it all kinds of potential harms, as well as meaning and delight of the highest kind, each because of the other. This does not mean that we need to excuse negative behaviour in others or in ourselves, or that we should not try to make amends or improve as people.

Sometimes relationships end badly, and it is not necessarily any one person's fault. Trying to discover who was the 'bad guy' in a relationship is a one-sided game, yet many people, both men and women, seem to want to engage in this type of blaming, as if life, and love, were so simple. This is partly because we have been encouraged to look for and trust in a single other far too much – as if there is one person out there who can truly see us and redeem us, who can complete our lives. And if it goes wrong, we must 'hate' them for betraying our fantasy.

Sometimes, perhaps, there is a singular loved other, but even if you do find such a person, the act of being with them is an ongoing, daily commitment, not something that is straightforward or easy. A person is not a thing. A real relationship is not a commodity. Life is frequently difficult and unfair and we are all often in need of reality checks. To expect one person to be, for example, your lover, friend, carer, bank manager, cleaner, childminder, chef and therapist is a tall order. It is obvious that any long-term, serious relationship, however funny and joyful it might be, is always in need of hard work. This type of commitment is often at odds with a culture that privileges short-termism, replacing things that aren't broken, and a general atmosphere of faddishness, ease and comfort. While for a period in the twentieth century, the couple or the family came to be seen by those on the left as traditional or oppressive (and oppressive *because* traditional), and indeed in many ways it was stifling and masked all kinds of violence, the family can also be understood as a bastion of resistance against the outside world: if the state goes mad, if institutions start to make little sense, if what you're being taught makes no sense, the family can bring you back down to earth with love and understanding.

When working well, the family can provide sanity, protection and normality, a small haven amid chaos. A politics that seeks to displace or destroy the family will not, in any case, last long. It no longer seems to me to be politically radical to advocate for destroying, or 'abolishing', the family. On the contrary, eliminating the family very much suits an economy and a culture that create and prey upon the isolated, atomic individual. The couple too can be a 'secret society'.[8]

The world is often insanity-inducing. In the modern era we are surrounded by demented machines and encouraged to be always connected. It is not clear, to me at least, whether technology has made relationships easier or harder, though my bet is on the latter. As the thinker and priest Ivan Illich once wrote, in defending a notion of austerity (not the economic policy beloved of post-crash neoliberal governments, but rather a form of personal relatedness): '[Austerity] is the fruit of an apprehension that things or tools could destroy rather than enhance *eutrapelia* (or graceful playfulness) in personal relations.'⁹ Austerity here is the turning away from distraction towards the things that really, ultimately matter: our affections and relations, our conversations, our difficulties and shared reality.

It is in the spirit of 'graceful playfulness' that this book is conceived, against the potential domination of our capacity for relationships by a cruel culture. Some of the text draws on the ways in which men talk about themselves and women online, and includes reflections on online discussions, pornography and internet dating, among other things. Like Illich, I think this technology threatens to take us away from the playfulness and risk of life, while simultaneously inducing various unhelpful kinds of suspicion and fear. If you want to punish someone for a perceived harm, for example, the internet is a blunt but effective tool, an extra-judicial weapon in the war of the sexes. It's not clear, though, how easy or possible it is to use it responsibly, particularly where matters of the heart are concerned.

Today the internet exists as a gigantic repository of all of the terrible things that people are capable of thinking. We are spying and being spied upon. It is not a particularly carefree or joyful medium. We often run the risk of our tools using us, of negatively conditioning our attitude towards each other. The internet often presents a false and unbalanced picture of how things really are: yet there we also find our desires mirrored back at us, sometimes horrifyingly so. The internet has made us in some ways less open to random encounters, to chance, to risk — yet life is made up of these things. As the Savage says in *Brave New World* : 'But I don't want comfort. I want God, I want poetry, I want real danger, I want freedom, I want goodness. I want sin . . . I'm claiming the right to be unhappy.'¹⁰

Human beings have apparently not yet transcended their historic human desire for misery, which sometimes comes in the form of the opposite sex. But what, if anything, has changed in the past couple of decades? When I was a teenager, people generally met each other romantically in real life, randomly, often through school, college or the pub. The 1990s was a much more 'in-person' decade than the 2010s and perhaps the 2020s will turn out to be, even leaving aside the pandemic lockdowns. Drinking and drugs were perhaps more collective experiences than they are now, and there was a kind of gleeful sort of 'equality of the debauched' that occurred at a particular historical moment between young men and women. 'Ladettes', girls who would drink and be as vulgar as their male friends, and 'lads' would battle it out to be as excessive and silly as possible.

I loved being a tomboy and 'one of the lads', even if the alcohol habit turned out to be a hard one to break. This kind of no-holds-barred, mutual mockery wasn't particularly dignified, but it did mark an interesting turn towards a certain kind of social equality. Without wishing to mythicize the recent past, there was definitely a sense in which we understood that we were all worthy of a decent piss-taking, and that it was positive to laugh at oneself as well as others, especially if done in good humour. I continue to believe that men and women must be able to mock each other for their excesses as individuals or as a group without hating each other, and without taking disproportionate offence. I honestly think this kind of ribbing operates precisely as a kind of safety value to ward off greater misery and resentment. There is so much affection in being able to laugh at oneself and each other: we cannot carry on being so scared of hurting each other that everyone ends up even more upset! To stay on the side of reality (and sanity) it is worth listening to others when they tell you how they see you, rather than trying to force them into going along with whatever idealized image you might have of yourself. Everyone is an idiot, sometimes.

The pre-internet era wasn't all good of course, and there might well be some positive reasons to celebrate this subsequent, more cautious, less hedonistic, era. But we might note at least how times change, subtly, and ask how men and women can get along today, how we can be more honest with each other, kinder but also more realistic, and yet still more playful and graceful. How can we learn to love and respect each other when these eternal values seem so discouraged by the broader culture? Whether we imagine we live at the end of history, or in the middle of late capitalism, or in the midst of the collapse of liberalism, or however else this current period could be conceived, it is certainly no exaggeration to say that such values are neglected. It is possible to ignore the dominant culture, of course, and many people have turned their back on it in the name of religion, tradition or other ideas of collective well-being. But this takes courage, and the desire to see beyond the narrow bounds of life as it is presented to us by the mainstream.

A brief note regarding terminology: throughout this book I use the word 'sex' rather than 'gender' to refer to men and women, and in places I also use the word 'sex' to refer to the physical act. The meaning of the word should hopefully be clear from context. I think the word 'gender' has in recent decades often been used to avoid using the word 'sex', due to the latter's potentially 'embarrassing' other meaning. But this polite use of 'gender' has increasingly caused new difficulties in the way we understand the world, as I will try to explain in part in what follows.

1.   Modern Man in Search of a Role

> Women think men should go to therapy. And men think
> men should lift weights. In fact, men should read all
> seven volumes of Proust's magnum opus *À la recherche
> du temps perdu* in the original French.
>
> Jack, on Twitter[1]

Why did I write this book? Partly because I have been personally and politically disturbed by the divisions created by media and technology between men and women in my own lifetime. Partly because I feel that men and women have had their lives reduced to generalizations by a media that loves sweeping claims; I think that these claims don't accord in the slightest with the complex reality of our lives. It has become very easy to speak cynically and dismissively of a group of people on the basis of taking minor examples and acting as if they apply to everyone included. There are, furthermore, in the current understanding of the world, some groups one is 'allowed' to denigrate, and others it is forbidden to criticize. The most oppressed groups according to today's logic are those that suffer, or have suffered in the past, by virtue of their identity. Those who want to make the world a better place — and who doesn't? — if they are not themselves members of oppressed groups are encouraged to be 'allies' to these groups, be they trans women, the descendants of enslaved people, or other people marked by poor treatment. And why shouldn't there be a historical shift in who receives preferential treatment?

The problem comes when there is, in effect, according to this schema, the implicit idea of a finite (or small) amount of suffering. That there is only enough sympathy to go round for whichever group is deemed to deserve it in the present moment. This quantitative image of pain would mean that some people do not suffer *even when they do*, which is to say, their suffering does not count for anything. So men, to take the theme of this book, cannot truly suffer, even when they do, because their suffering is not as real or important as the suffering of others.

At the same time, there is a strong moral strain in some of today's politics, which may not only be misplaced, but, in actuality, actively dangerous. There can exist a kind of cruelty when one is convinced that one is behaving in the name of the 'good', that is to say, when one believes one is helping those who should be helped. As philosopher Judith Shklar puts it:

> One of our political actualities is that the victims of political torture and injustice are often no better than their tormentors. They are only waiting to change places with the latter . . . even at the cost of misanthropy, one cannot afford to pretend that victimhood improves anyone in any way. If we do not remember that anyone can be a victim, and if we allow hatred for torture, or pity for pain, to blind us, we will unwittingly aid the torturers of tomorrow by overrating the victims of today. One may be too easily tempted to think of all victims as equally innocent because there cannot, by definition, be a voluntary victim. That may have the consequence of promoting an endless exchange of cruelties between alternating tormentors and victims.[2]

Victimhood today has paradoxically become a very powerful tool, and a potentially vicious one. It is far, far harder but absolutely necessary to begin not with the desire to rank victims, but rather with the understanding that everyone suffers, and to try to work out how best to minimize that suffering *for everybody*, which requires careful, and adult, negotiation. Repaying one group for the suffering of another will only result in a backlash even worse than the original harm. If men have benefitted in the past, let us imagine a kinder way of redistributing their gains for all, rather than entering into an 'endless exchange of cruelties'. Let women be the bigger man.

I have a hope that, following a great deal of bitterness in recent years, men and women can reconcile on the basis of a renewed and greater understanding of one another. I want us to forgive one another, where possible, to be reunited, and to enjoy life in each other's company – or without each other, if that is what we might want. I hope that we can live in such a way that the differences between men and women can be admitted *where it is important to admit them* – without these differences interfering with our larger commitments to love and respect each other as human beings in the world. We are not the same. It is pointless and ultimately more damaging to act as if we are: this does not mean, though, that we cannot do and love many of the same things, and each other. We should not be tricked into scapegoating one another: we all lose if we do this.

So, what *do* men want? Asking the general question of 'what a man wants' or even what any individual man 'wants' is, naturally, a fool's errand. It's the same problem Sigmund Freud had when he asked in a letter to Marie Bonaparte in 1925 'what does a woman want?' Almost a hundred years later, in turning the question around, it is obvious that there is no one good or simple answer, just as Freud could not solve his reverse enquiry. But in the spirit of play – graceful or otherwise – let us pretend that desire is somehow capable of answering when a simple question is put to it.

When I asked male friends what they thought men wanted, they answered with, among other things, the following: 'Tell me when you find out', 'A pleasant woman', 'To be left alone', 'Pussy', 'To hang out with my male friends', 'To be a good man', 'A shed', 'A woman who will let me be myself', 'An easy life', 'Nigella Lawson', 'Why are you asking me? I'm a rubbish man', and 'A beer'.

But some people *do* imagine there is a simple answer. There exists today a whole industry dedicated to attempting to tell men what they *should* want. Masculinity is big business. Various books and websites tell you quite clearly how to be a man. Some are pick-up-artist manuals, which is to say, books that teach you how to successfully flirt with and 'hook up' with women. Some are guidebooks on how to be more masculine, and how to get fit through weight-lifting and other kinds of physical training. Some are reflective accounts of the trouble with masculinity, and some are somewhere in between. Many of these accounts of 'how to be a man' pitch themselves more or less aggressively against the 'feminizing' (and therefore) enervating aspects of today's culture.

Whatever we think of the masculinity industry, the current demonization of men is a negative situation for everyone. It breeds massive amounts of resentment on both sides and closes off certain possibilities for, among other things, a more generous, understanding and playful relation between the sexes. When we look at the recent rise of self-help thinkers such as Jordan Peterson who appeal mainly to young men, we see, in part, something of a cultural need being filled for a father figure to the masses.

Peterson inhabits a certain image of the patriarch: a smartly dressed, almost 1950s-era older man who offers insight and takes responsibility for guiding the youth. Peterson, who in his 2018 bestseller, *12 Rules for Life: An Antidote to Chaos*, promises to teach you how to avoid 'pathways to Hell', symbolizes a certain need for direction, which is often otherwise absent in the wider culture, or in young people's family lives. His appeal lies in his synthetic wisdom – a combination of Christianity, liberal values, Jungian ideas and a confrontation with suffering: 'To stand up straight with your shoulders back is to accept the terrible responsibility of life, with eyes wide open'.[3] Many people, it seems, desire the kind of certainty that comes from someone saying basic things in a stern manner: 'Tidy your room!' or 'Sort your life out!'

Could Peterson only have been a man? 'Tidy your room!' is also the kind of thing that mothers, perhaps especially, say to their teenage children. Young women are surely in as much need of guidance as young men, and some men would do well to listen to older, wiser women. Yet, as Ed West asks, 'how come there has never been a female Jordan Peterson?'[4] Writer Mary Harrington points out in response that 'a female Jordan Peterson would have to talk about motherhood. But the paradox is that those who are in the thick of motherhood don't have time to be Jordan Peterson.'[5] Harrington goes on to suggest that a female Jordan Peterson could be found among the ranks of women who have already raised their children, and that we should 'platform more grannies'.[6]

Part of the project of reconciliation I'm interested in here might well involve 'more grannies': the way in which the collective wisdom of the elderly is side-lined by a culture obsessed with youth, novelty and transience is truly terrible. Mothers, and older women, are often ignored in political discourse, or dismissed horribly by both young men and young women.

My book is not really about how to be more manly, nor will it particularly help, I suspect, any woman seeking to improve her relationship with any particular man, at least not in any straightforward way. It is partly philosophical, partly observational, and partly a work of cultural criticism. I've looked at some extreme aspects of male life the better to understand how some men think, and what this tells us more broadly about what dialogue might be possible in the future. During the research for this book I found it fascinating to observe, online and off, what men talk about when they talk about themselves, and what they say about women, particularly when they don't think women are listening.

I am honestly not entirely sure that women *should* know what is said about them out of earshot, but in the spirit of a certain kind of bloody-minded enlightenment, I decided to find out. There is a lot I miss out – I don't really talk about men and sports, for example, though there would be a lot to say about masculinity and football, in particular. This book was written in the UK, and my examples are largely drawn from Western countries. It is largely about the relationship – or lack thereof – between men and women, therefore it does not discuss male homosexuality in any real depth.

My text therefore focuses on men, women, heterosexuality, and, as we shall see, *heterosociality*. When I say we live in a 'heterosocial' world, I mean that the sexes are mixed almost everywhere in cultural, daily and economic life, with major historical consequences: the question of how men and women should interact at work following #MeToo, for example, or the ongoing question today of whether there are spaces and realms, such as toilets, changing rooms, sports, prisons and shelters, that should continue to be segregated by biological sex.

'Hetero*sociality*' here means something a lot broader than the more common word 'hetero*sexuality*'. The social includes the sexual, but is not reducible to it. We are 'heterosocial' all the time in the modern world, whether we like it or not. Women have definitely entered political, cultural and economic spheres. There is an incomplete equality at work, and our differences and similarities are in something of an uneasy stand-off where we don't always know what it means to be a man or a woman, or, at least, we don't always know when these things should matter or not. There is no going back, I think, to a more segregated world, though separatism is a partial option (or desire) for a very few men, as we will see. I also don't think the solution to our disagreements lies in more technology, and I am very wary of transhumanist or futuristic suggestions for solving the 'problem' of sexual difference, i.e. artificial wombs. If anything, I propose simply a certain acceptance of the world we have, the world we share, the world we live in together.

'Toxic masculinity', a phrase emerging in the 1980s and 1990s which saw an explosion of use from around 2014 onwards, seeks to capture the idea that certain kinds of male behaviour are poisonous, to men themselves as well as to others. These would include, among other things, misogyny, homophobia, an acceptance of violence as natural, and male dominance in general. The idea of 'toxic masculinity' is today, however, often invoked generally to describe and name everything from men speaking over women to the murderous rage of a tiny number of men. As Maya Salem put it in *The New York Times*, toxic masculinity is 'what can come of teaching boys that they can't express emotion openly; that they have to be "tough all the time"; that anything other than that makes them "feminine" or weak'.[7]

In previous eras there were different ways of speaking about men. We might have talked about a family man, a fancy man, a ladies' man, a cad, a rogue, a man of the world, a man of his day, yesterday's man, or a man of his word. Today we often lack these principles of discrimination and discernment, encouraged to tar all men with the same brush and operating in a permanent state of vigilance, shuddering at the merest hint of supposed male 'toxicity'. But what in any case could this toxicity be? The word itself comes from a Greek word meaning 'poison', relating especially to arrows, and we can also hear echoes of the dangers of nuclear waste, a substance that must be contained at the risk of spreading harmful particles. To describe masculinity as 'toxic' is to suggest that not only have men been poisoned, but that they are extending their poison to the rest of society. Men might still be overall seen as more trustworthy than women in some contexts, but a poison gas is seeping out everywhere. Masculinity is contagious and deadly.

But what is the remedy? There is a tension here at the heart of the situation. Either men cannot or should not be masculine at all, which might entail them becoming 'more like women' in a stereotypical sense, which is to say more empathetic, more sensitive and so on. Or they should be adopting different kinds of masculinity that are not so 'toxic'. Or men could instead simply refuse the idea that any kind of masculinity is toxic at all, and assert that they have a right to behave however they like. We see all of these options playing out across different areas of life, and those of different political persuasions have strong feelings about whether men should behave in a 'modern' way, or whether male nature has something unshakeably 'masculine', that is to say, rough, about it.

One example of male toxicity is indicated by the term 'mansplaining'. As Lara Rutherford-Morrison puts it:

When a man 'mansplains' something to a woman, he interrupts or speaks over her to explain something that she already knows – indeed, something in which she may already be an expert – on the assumption that he must know more than she does. In many cases, the explanation has to do specifically with things that are unique to women – their bodies, their experiences, their lives. When men interrupt or presume to correct a woman who is speaking of her own experience or expertise, they are implying that she is ignorant, that she is incapable of having authoritative knowledge. They are saying, essentially, 'Shh. I know best.'[8]

There is no doubt that this kind of 'talking-over' happens, and not only by men over women. But I wonder if sometimes an enthusiasm for talking is misconstrued as patronizing or arrogant speech. Is the issue with 'mansplaining', the explanation itself, or rather a certain performance of it – so that the criticism is really directed against men who are doing it badly rather than the act itself? Women, like all sentient beings, enjoy a well-told story. Would that we could all learn to entertain each other to the best of our ability. Sometimes it is genuinely delightful to hear someone share their knowledge, even if it's something you already have a good idea about. If we all had more time to talk and listen, and did not feel so pressured to speak, conversation would undoubtedly be greatly improved.

Men also stand accused, perhaps more light-heartedly, of 'manspreading', sitting with their legs widely apart on public transport and crushing those sitting beside them, as if possessed of such great manliness that they would hurt themselves if their legs were any closer together. Other negative man-related terms have emerged in recent years, such as 'mentrification', whereby, according to Van Badham:

> If 'gentrification' describes the process by which one 'improves' a place so it 'conforms to middle-class taste', mentrification achieves an equal status transformation by taking the history of female participation and achievement, and festooning its narrative with phalluses.[9]

Some of these neologisms might raise a smile, others might seem unfair. But no discussion of any of these shots fired could be complete without a discussion of #MeToo, the largest wide-scale attack on male power in recent history.

It's 2018. #MeToo is in full swing, after the resurrection of the term in October 2017 by Hollywood and celebrity actors, who took the phrase from Tarana Burke, an activist and community organizer who had first used it in 2006 to highlight the sexual abuse suffered by poor black women and children. Through paralegal means, such as internet denunciations and anonymous stories, alongside personal stories and the hashtag, many men in positions of power across every industry are named as having behaved inappropriately, sexually or otherwise, and, in many cases, they are usurped from their jobs and, in some cases, socially ostracized. There have since been a few high-profile prison sentences handed out to, among others, Harvey Weinstein and cult leader Keith Raniere.

Some men were, unsurprisingly, perturbed by #MeToo. Writing for the *Washington Post*, dating coach Harris O'Malley concludes that 'the only line separating a co-worker and a harassment suit is convenience.'[10] There's a popular internet meme on this point that shows characters at an office. In one box titled 'appropriate', a good-looking man is saying, 'Looking good, Susan', to which the female worker responds, 'Aww, you're sweet.' In the second box, marked 'inappropriate', an overweight man in glasses makes the same compliment to Susan, to which she is seen to respond by picking up the phone and calling Human Resources, no doubt to report her colleague for sexual harassment. Context is all. Life is full of misunderstandings, confusion and mistakes. Ascribing malign intention to anything that upsets you will generate more fearfulness. How can a man tell if a woman is interested in being approached? Well, often he cannot. It is far safer to stay away. In this respect, men are not wrong to be wary of taking on the mentorship of young women, for example, or to be increasingly careful of what they say and do at work (one 2010 study found that two-thirds of men shied away from mentoring junior women for fear that others would suspect sexual intentions).[11] Constructing harsh rules for the ways in which men and women should interact at work, for example, might prevent the most egregious types of antisocial behaviour, or it might not.

The #MeToo event has not proceeded, however, without a certain push-back from women. A letter was published in France, signed by Catherine Deneuve and many other female luminaries. It stated, among other things, the following:

> As women, we don't recognize ourselves in this feminism that, beyond the denunciation of abuses of power, takes the face of a hatred of men and sexuality. We believe that the freedom to say 'no' to a sexual proposition cannot exist without the freedom to bother. And we consider that one must know how to respond to this freedom to bother in ways other than by closing ourselves off in the role of the prey [. . .] Incidents that can affect a woman's body do not necessarily affect her dignity and must not, as difficult as they can be, necessarily make her a perpetual victim. Because we are not reducible to our bodies. Our inner freedom is inviolable. And this freedom that we cherish is not without risks and responsibilities.[12]

This image of freedom is absolutely at odds with another dominant character in today's social pantheon that we have already met – the victim. Are women fundamentally free, or are they not? If they are not, who has responsibility for them? If something bad happens at the hands of a man, does that define who that woman is, and, if so, for how long? From a philosophical and feminist point of view, I think it would be entirely inadequate to deny that women are fundamentally free – free not only to respond to men, free to follow their own desire, and to reject the logic of fear and victimhood that diminishes their capacity to be in the world. Let us be clear: this freedom hits a wall when male violence is at its most extreme, when women are hurt and killed by men. It is imperative that we find every possible solution to the problem of male violence, beginning, above all, with prevention. We all, no doubt, agree on this. The question is deciding how best to collectively achieve it.

In this regard, the #MeToo moment could be read from one angle as historically inevitable, as part of the usual process of the shift in social mores that periodically occurs. But it also revealed the destructive power of the internet in relation to names – once you put someone's name out there attached to an unsavoury allegation, you have no control over the extent to which that claim spreads nor can you contain the effects it might have on someone's life. Some accusers no doubt justly felt that their complaints could not be handled legally for various reasons, therefore there was no other option than to make them online – but the court of public opinion, where many men stand accused of serious offences, often anonymously and with no way of verifying them, is an extremely rough system. The opportunities for malevolence are high, and the rewards uncertain.

Other types of men have also come under attack. We have seen the repeated demonization of so-called 'incels' – involuntary celibates – men who do not have a girlfriend or sexual relations with women (interestingly, though, the term was originally coined by a woman).[13] These young men meet online, although their forums are frequently shut down, to discuss their predicament and to share memes. Described by Kate Manne as 'a vivid symptom of a much broader and deeper cultural phenomenon. [Incels] crystallize some men's toxic sense of entitlement to have people look up to them steadfastly, with a loving gaze, admiringly – and to target and even destroy those who fail, or refuse to do so.'[14] Several murders have been pinned to 'incels', including Elliot Rodger, who killed six people by stabbing and shooting in California in 2014, and Alex Minassian, who drove a van into pedestrians, killing ten people in Toronto in 2018.

The vast majority of incels are not, however, murderers. Wanting to be loved is a deeply human desire. When these young men come together to commiserate online they are not only sharing their resentment at being unable to find love, but are creating a community for outsiders. Society loves to pile on its 'losers', but as Alex Lee Moyer's 2020 documentary about US incels *TFW No GF* shows, many of these young men are economically deprived, living in miserable small towns without much hope of secure employment, let alone many of the other trappings of middle-class life and future prospects, and yet they can be charming and funny and inventive online. Moyer's documentary was attacked for humanizing the 'incel community', but let's put this another way: is it better to understand the men we fear, or is it better to isolate and ostracize them further? A society that understood brokenness and the potential for violence might not be able to eliminate it completely, but it might do a better job of reintegrating those who stand on the brink by embracing and helping them to feel less alone.

Anybody who cares about humanity as such should also be concerned about the pain of men – not least because how else are we collectively supposed to minimize this pain, the better to prevent men from passing it on – to themselves, to each other, to women?

There is currently a major drugs crisis in the USA that largely afflicts poor and working-class men and women, with 72,000 people dying as a result of it in 2019 – 70 per cent of whom were men.[15] 'Men's rights activists' often seek to highlight male suffering of this kind. MRAs, as they are usually known, are part of the 'men's rights movement', which is frequently accused of 'male supremacy', misogyny and hatred, though I don't think the entire movement can be reduced to this by any means. In reality, it is hard to see where 'male privilege' is supposed to lie, particularly when looking at the life chances of poor and working-class men.

MRAs can be found online in the 'manosphere', myriad online sites dedicated to all things manly. Here you will come across pick-up artists, the no-fap (anti-masturbation/anti-porn) movement, multiple weight-lifting and gym communities, and various sites that encourage discipline and fitness in the name of refusing the ongoing 'emasculation' of today's man.

There are also male separatists of a kind, as we will see. In particular MGTOW, 'Men Going Their Own Way', a movement that claims that historically 60 per cent of men never had children of their own. MGTOW followers tend to opt out of what they see as the 'parasitic' nature of contemporary dating, which they consider to be unfair: men, they say, accurately or otherwise, are still supposed to pick up the bill in return for a measly chance at sex or a relationship. Why bother? Instead MGTOW members celebrate male achievement beyond the family. Their heroes are, among others, Tesla, Beethoven, Galileo and Jesus Christ.

Some men today pride themselves on their physical prowess, spending time at the gym or engaging in highly physical sports in their spare time. This is perhaps evidence of a war against our sedentary, informational age. Some men want a life without women, others just want to get fit and stay healthy: and why not? But is this all there is to contemporary masculinity?

We have lost sight today of the possibility of linking masculinity to *goodness* – and this, above all, is what I want to defend. How to get there? We could, as Grayson Perry suggests, begin by questioning 'outdated' versions of masculinity.[16] We could say, as he does, that masculinity 'needs to change' because most versions of it are a 'blight' on society; or we could shift a little and say that perhaps we need to resurrect what was good about older kinds of masculinity in the name of a different image of the present and future. Many men are *already* good, which is to say they look after themselves and others, care for their families, sacrifice their time and energy to making the world a better place for all: it is unfair and untrue therefore to damn men and masculinity *as such*.

The general social attitude today is, however, to be worried that masculinity is damaging to both boys and men and girls and women. The American Psychological Association *Guidelines for Psychological Practice with Boys and Men* (2018), states that 'In Western culture, the dominant ideal of masculinity has moved from an upper-class aristocratic image to a more rugged and self-sufficient ideal.'[17] The APA stresses that these ideals are in any case damaging stereotypes, and might 'potentially alienate sexual- and gender-minority men from a complete male identity' as well as 'ostracize some gay, bisexual, transgender, and gender-nonconforming individuals'.[18] While noting that 'although privilege has not applied to all boys and men in equal measure, in the aggregate, males experience a greater degree of social and economic power than girls and women in a patriarchal society,' the authors go on to add that 'male privilege often comes with a cost in the form of adherence to sexist ideologies designed to maintain male power that also restrict men's ability to function adaptively'.[19]

Following the historic, economic and social 'masculinization' of women (women's entry into many of the worlds that used to belong solely to men), we now sometimes also witness the 'feminizing' of men, in the form of an imposed guilt upon boys and men merely for behaving in 'masculine', that is to say today, in 'negative' ways – being boisterous, loud, domineering, and so on. Certain kinds of behaviour come to be rewarded over others – we can see this all the way to the job market where many economies have themselves become 'feminized', that is to say, less physical, more dependent on traditionally 'feminine' skills such as communication and sociability. Western economies largely do not require large amounts of physical labour. This has an impact on the values of our culture at large. If it is positive that men are less 'manly' than they were in the past, then that is part of our cultural evolution. But far better to note what has been lost, than to pretend that this is the only way things must henceforth be.

In the West, compared to the past and to many other societies, we see a generalized abdication of male instruction, and a lack of initiation rituals in the passage from boyhood to manhood. If masculinity is in trouble today, it is because our understanding of humanity *as a whole* is in trouble. What would, instead, a masculinity directly related to an idea of the *good* look like today? It can only begin by resurrecting the necessity of virtue as such, which is to say to recognize the capacity of men to be good in the first place. In order for the question of the good to even be asked, we have to return to older ideas of virtue. Boys and men must be *allowed* to be good, to become better, and be celebrated for doing so.

So, there is, it seems to me, this very deep and ancient question at the heart of what it means to be a man or a woman, namely, what it means to be a *good* man and a *good* woman. This is by no means an easy question when today there either seems to be no answer or too many answers to it. The question of sex *is* a question of morality, though this is something we tend to scoff at these days – 'As if there's any one way to be a good man!', 'How could we know!', 'F★★k off! No one tells me how to live!' It sounds religious or conservative to link one's moral being to one's sex: it is to be anti-modern, regressive, restrictive, oppressive. Don't we live in an age in which we can choose how to live as individuals decoupled from our sex? Are we not sublimely, historically, free?

If we talk today about being a 'good man' we no doubt hear the shudder-inducing echo of an earlier, narrow, understanding of masculinity. We think of the punishment of men who failed to live up to an 'ideal'. But the emphasis here should be on trying to live as honestly and realistically as possible, not about living up to some impossible standard or imagining that there is one ideal way of being a man. For example, by learning *how* and *when* to use one's judgement and strength, both physical and mental, one also learns how not to *misuse* these things.

People are good men or women because they do good things, or try to, not because an individual says of themselves that they are 'good', or because they have the 'right line' on an issue. The question of what these 'good things' are is complicated, and must be discovered through trial and error, but we can begin from the assumption that we are all unlikely to find out what goodness is from a culture based, in the first place, on the manipulation of desires for negative ends – that is to say, an amoral consumerism that panders to our basest desires. In order then to discover what it means to be a good man or woman, we must question how the world today is sold to us, and need to be prepared to look at ourselves in the mirror without the protection of cynicism or the distraction of endless cover stories about how 'progressive' modern life is supposed to be.

In our age, the kind of 'freedom' offered by a hedonistic capitalism has tried to turn us all into something less than human. Rather, we are commodities of a kind, person-sized objects that sell themselves while simultaneously accumulating things. Our 'rewards', such as they are, tend to draw us deeper into the world of things, and often towards oblivion and distraction. In the realm of thought, social media has revealed that the punishments for disagreeing with others can be severe: it may be that we all need to get offline sooner rather than later, the better to remember who we are, and who our real friends are. We are often compelled to forget that free and simple pleasures – conversation, walking outside, being in nature – are also available to us. Beyond endless consumption, the nervous avoidance of serious questions, or a lack of confidence in how we handle ourselves, life can often be very beautiful. What it means to be a man, and what it means to be a woman, are precisely questions that are posed, implicitly or otherwise, in these sacred times and these elevating places. Only a cynical mindset seeks to diminish experiences that are open to all.

What then can and does this world tell us about men, and about the relationship between men and women? Humanity's break with nature appears to have been decisive – indeed, to even invoke 'nature' is to run the risk of falling into essentialism, the worst of all crimes today: 'You are saying something is a certain thing, and can't be another thing!' But part of accepting life and becoming mature is understanding and accepting what cannot be changed. Our culture often flinches from the idea that 'men' and 'women' can be defined, and that we can draw any conclusions about who we are from our biology. But we are, it must be admitted, *alive*, somewhere midway between nature and history. We are not virtual. We are real and embodied, despite dreams of artificial wombs, immortality, and other proposed technological 'solutions'.

Human beings are a sexually dimorphic species. Sexual difference is real. There has been a great deal of trepidation in saying this in recent years, and the costs for individuals and professionals who do so has sometimes been very high. But there is no third sex. Intersex conditions are extremely rare, and do not demonstrate that sex is a spectrum, as some suggest (the editors of *Scientific American* in 2017, for example, state that 'to varying extents, many of us are biological hybrids on a male–female continuum'[20]): on the contrary, intersex conditions prove that there are two sexes by virtue of being disruptions in the sexual development of male or female bodies.[21]

But being male or female need not be oppressive. How we decide to live out our lives as the sexed beings that we are is up to us. Gender is the name we give to the expectations society has of us. In recent years, however, the use of this word has shifted: we've moved from an idea of gender as something imposed from the outside (i.e. the expectation that girls/boys and men/women should behave in certain ways) to an idea of gender as something felt internally, or as something that could be claimed as an identity.

The first position understands that gender is something to *get beyond*, i.e. that we collectively need to open up the possibilities of expressing oneself however one wants, but this approach does not deny the underlying reality of sexual difference (important for, among other things, understanding how our bodies actually work). The second idea of gender is regressive, although it purports to be progressive: it says that if you like things typically associated with boys/girls or men/women then you must 'be' that identity. Keira Bell is a young woman who became a trans man then detransitioned. In December 2020, she won her case against the Tavistock Gender Identity Development Service, arguing that they had prescribed her puberty blockers without due consideration. Bell described her first appointment with the clinic at the age of sixteen in the following way: 'I had a one-hour appointment and it was very general, surface-level stuff. "What is your preferred name? Do you want to transition?" And a lot of stereotype talk about whether I played with boys' toys, preferred boys' clothes. There was no discussion about my sexuality.'[22]

I believe that the difference between the sexes is real and important on every level of our collective being. It is by understanding the fact that we are *in the first place* either male or female that we can then decide *how* to live out this fact, even if we decide to live as the opposite sex, or as no sex, or both. Sex has a historical as well as a biological reality. It is destructive to everyone to pretend that this isn't true.

Sexual difference is nevertheless always riven with possibility, not least because there is a limit to how much we can 'be like' the 'opposite' sex. We can mimic the social attributes and 'roles' of the sex which we are not, and indeed, much of the twentieth century was arguably devoted to *closing the gap* between what boys and girls, men and women could do and be, and who they could love. This was a major social project, often led by feminists, that sought to allow people to be whoever they want to be. This position did not seek to deny or escape biological reality, or to pretend that sexual difference didn't exist, but it did deny that anyone had to behave a certain way *because* of their sex.

When I was growing up, you did not have to be a boy to like toys, hobbies or jobs typically or historically associated with the male sex. And it didn't 'make you a girl' if you were a boy who liked sparkly things (many girls didn't like them either). The subsequent forgetting of sex, and the reinforcement of the idea that if you like 'boy' things then you must be one, has partly arisen because of an emphasis on individual identity, which takes us further away from who we are as a differentiated but collective social body.

Social media has encouraged people to present a 'shopping list' of aspects of their being, in place of developing personality or character. It is of course much easier to declare yourself as something novel than it is to dedicate years of your life to becoming a well-rounded individual, or a scholar, or an activist. Yet we do not, in reality, live as isolated 'identities' but instead exist in relation to people around us. Human beings are mimetic, which is to say, we copy and emulate each other constantly. Paradoxically, or rather perversely, this would include the social contagion of people who privilege individual identity – in many ways, this is another, somewhat detrimental, way of belonging, which involves copying what others do. Perhaps culture will swing back again soon to thinking and acting collectively and cooperatively, as opposed to encouraging the creation of millions of little islands.

We are all complicated beings with multiple desires, many of which conflict. Yet we are all also simply thrown into the world with a body we didn't choose. This is a shared experience, even as we might find ourselves alienated from the world and feel that we struggle alone. It is far kinder, in the end, to admit that life is hard for everyone, than it is to encourage individuals to feel like it is their fault alone that they feel bad. A greater shared understanding of the difficulties of life from childhood onwards would, paradoxically, encourage greater overall contentment.

Do we live in the time of the 'twilight of the penis'?[23] Or are men more dominant than ever? Do men and women love each other? Do we secretly hate each other? Or do we merely tolerate each other as nature plays merry tricks on us behind our backs? The questions posed by the great religious and mythical texts of the past are not so far removed from the twenty-first century as we might like to believe. There is, marvellously, very little new under the sun, which we all live under.

There are many strange and wonderful friendships and positive interactions of all kinds happening all the time between boys and girls and men and women. There are many more ways of loving and being together than the merely sexual, and affection beyond the romantic is, in some ways, more meaningful. Our age has pushed a simplistic version of erotic love as the most desirable way of being with another person at the expense of more lively and spirited communion.

For the Greeks, for example, the ludic (playful), was a kind of love all of its own. How delightful this is: to play is to have an entirely different relation to time beyond the one imposed by the clock, and by the obligation to work. It is imperative for the future of the species that we expand and develop new games to play with one another! We bond over games that we ourselves make up. Relationships between men and women can be flirtatious, amusing, amicable, thoughtful, compassionate, understanding, mutually baffling, and so on. I think we must try to open up the space for a kind of infinite play that at the same time is serious – serious in its playfulness. We too often forget the pleasure of play. Some games too have beautiful outcomes, and even just in the playing of them the present is rendered sublime.

Lately, an unforgiving strain of feminism has been pushed – though this feminism doesn't bear much resemblance to the sort I grew up with. The kind I remember encouraged both girls and boys not to feel hemmed in by gender roles. It did not 'blame' people for the sex they were.

To be a man today, however, is a guilt-ridden business. To live guiltily, however, is not a useful or a beneficial way for anyone to live. It generates resentment in men, who, quite rightly, do not want to submit to an apologetic existence, and creates confusion in women, who want men to acknowledge *both* their capacity for harm and their capacity for goodness. Guilt produces nothing of any use for society if it doesn't change how we treat each other. On its own, it just doesn't do anything, and even creates greater misery. The assumption of men's guilt merely serves to delay a conversation and a dialogue that would arguably benefit us all. While this is a book, then, *about* men, it is also about the ongoing and always improvable relationship between men and women.

The final word in the phrase 'what do men want?' opens up the realm of desire, which is often shrouded, for good reason, in great mystery, promise and even a kind of terror. We often want things that are bad for us. We do not often know what it is we do want, and how this relates to what might be good for us, or for humanity as a whole. How many people, let alone men today, could say with any certainty that they knew and understood what desire was, let alone their own stake in it?

In 1997, John Carlin wrote in the *Independent* about a new course running at Hobart and William Smith Colleges, New York, entitled 'Men and Masculinity'. Women signed up in great numbers, just as they did to all 500 courses on the topic of masculinity given in the US during this period. Carlin suggests that in the end the answer to the question of what a man wants is, in fact, clear: a pair of Dockers trousers. At this time 70 per cent of US men owned a pair: 'Buying Dockers pants allows [the man] to satisfy a powerful craving to be one of the guys; to belong to the large extended club of like-minded, similarly confused, subtly attractive men.'[24] So, if we wanted one answer to the question of what men want, it would be a pair of trousers.

If only everything were so simple.

In his 1979 book, *The Culture of Narcissism*, Christopher Lasch, one of the great cultural historians of the twentieth century, as prescient as he was incisive, analyses the 'battle of the sexes', suggesting that capitalism has shifted from a paternalistic and familial form to a managerial, bureaucratic system of 'almost total control'.[25] Chivalry has collapsed, sex has been liberated from its former constraints, sexual pleasure has become an end in itself and personal relations have become emotionally overloaded. Furthermore, what has simultaneously transpired is an 'irrational male response to the emergence of the liberated woman'.[26] Having been stripped of their historical role of protecting women, Lasch suggests that men assert their residual desire for domination in violent fantasies: 'from reverence to rape', as one study he mentions puts it. 'Men no longer treat women as ladies', he notes, mournfully.[27] In Lasch's account, the proximity of the sexes induced by capitalist liberation has generated new forms of potential harm. How much more accurate his insights seem in a world of dating apps, and the great levelling of the sexes to the status of neutered, competitive beings.

Lasch (at the end of the 1970s) claimed that women have good reason to resent men: 'the resentment of women against men for the most part has solid roots in the discrimination and sexual danger to which women are constantly exposed'.[28] On the contrary, he thought, male resentment of women 'appears deeply irrational'. Lasch suggested that 'a thoroughgoing transformation of our

social arrangements remains a possibility', and that 'a socialist revolution would abolish the new paternalism'.[29] Perhaps Lasch was
too hopeful, and I could be wrong, but I don't think we are on the
cusp of a socialist revolution in the West. Whatever the current
uneasy amalgam of capitalism, liberal democracy and culture
wars might be called, I don't think it's going anywhere fast. All we
can really do is navigate it together as best we can. I do, however,
agree with Lasch when he concludes that the abolition of sexual
tensions is an 'unworthy goal': which is to say it would be
impossible, and perhaps even undesirable, to abolish disagreements between the sexes completely. As Lasch says, 'the point is
to live with them more gracefully than we have lived with them
in the past'.[30]

Despite everything, men and women still *just about* want to be
together. While the number of marriages has hit an all-time
low, nevertheless just over half (51 per cent) of the 2017 UK
population were married and the majority (61.4 per cent) of the
population aged sixteen years and over in England and Wales
were living in a couple in 2017.[31]

In the end, men and women can and already do care about each
other. We are not mortal enemies. We can't do without each
other, whoever we are, and we can restore the recognition of the
cosmic wonder of difference, to revere and enjoy each other with
humour and grace. We should be wary of those who seek to generate resentment by pitting men and women against each other.

Let us begin: in order to get to a kinder, wiser, more enchanted
place, we must think carefully about and accept responsibility for
our decisions, whether they be for friendship, sex, marriage and/
or children, while at the same time acknowledging a certain
unknowability, a deep enigma, at the heart of any and all of these
aspirations. But we shouldn't be afraid. We must speak and listen
carefully, face difficult questions about desire, and find joy and
pleasure and absurdity wherever we can together, while we can.

2. What is the Patriarchy?

The courage to be logical – the courage to name – would
require that we admit to ourselves that males and males
only are the originators, planners, controllers,
and legitimators of patriarchy.

Mary Daly, *Gyn/Ecology*[1]

The internet, and the consumerism that surrounds and is supported by it, has, in recent years, been full of admonitions against this thing called 'patriarchy' (or, more often, 'the patriarchy'). There are tote bags available with slogans such as 'Hex the patriarchy', 'Grab them by the patriarchy', 'My favourite season is the fall of the patriarchy', 'Fuck the patriarchy', 'Smash the patriarchy', 'Trample patriarchy' (a unicorn stands on a skull), 'R.I.P. patriarchy', 'Not today, patriarchy', 'Less patriarchy, more cupcakes', 'Smashing the patriarchy is my cardio', 'The patriarchy isn't going to fight itself', 'Pizza not patriarchy', and so on. 'The patriarchy' is, then, unambiguously, a bad thing, according to several bags.

But what is being referred to here? Are all men members of the patriarchy by default, or is it made manifest in certain behaviours performed by individual men? What about those terms I mentioned above, particularly 'mansplaining' and 'manspreading'? Patriarchy in action? These words describe certain kinds of behaviours negatively associated with men: they are perhaps annoying. But 'patriarchy' hints at something much more structural, much deeper, much more awful: 'men are its agents,' as

Daly says. Patriarchy, then, is a kind of monster, and men its minions.

A 'patriarch' perhaps appears in our mind's eye as a stern, possibly religious, figure. Abraham, Isaac, Jacob, a man who heads a family, someone who lays down the law, who decides what reality is, what women's role is, a man who determines human history. 'The patriarchy' in this analysis looms large as a structure of being, a system of rules and governance. Men do things. Men own things. In this model, women are property, therefore men own (or ought to own) women.

In reality, there is today a crisis of actual fathers – but we nevertheless feel still that we are governed by invisible 'father-structures', the ghosts of daddy past, *paterfamilias*. 'Patriarchy' is often invoked to explain the way the world is, to name an unfair hierarchy governed by male strength and the neglect and abuse of women, the theft of their knowledge and property. Patriarchy purports to identify the relations of property under which we live, and have lived for centuries. The word conjures images of the inescapable and long-term oppression and subordination of women by men; of asset ownership right down to the wombs and children of women; of moral dominance by men and the exclusion of women from public life and education.

But are men today still bearers of patriarchy? Do they perform it, intentionally or otherwise? Or do individual men merely benefit from it, receiving free symbolic advantage from a larger image of 'man' as superior? How does 'male privilege' relate to other factors, such as class? The attack on patriarchy in its sloganeering form makes it sound like some Lovecraftian monster, rising up from behind a series of tall, horribly phallic buildings, ready to steal women's time, enjoyment and wealth. Patriarchy is the name for something or someone we don't necessarily fully understand but know we do not like. It has a factual dimension – statistics – but also a mythical one. We cannot in fact 'smash' or 'fuck' or 'trample' the patriarchy, because it is not a being, but rather the structure of a certain *kind* of being, that is to say, how a society is organized. But organized by whom? Transmitted how? How and why have some – or many – women gone along with it?

In 2004's *The Will to Change: Men, Masculinity and Love*, a feminist book written to improve men, bell hooks (who deliberately uses a capital-free pseudonym) suggests that the battle against patriarchy must begin at home, with individual men and boys. Focusing on boyhood, she envisages a manhood that is less about violence and death than about intimacy, joy and connection.[2] With hooks we are back to the question of the family and the father once again. Love and connection are absolutely critical to everyone's upbringing. They do indeed make it possible for particular men to refuse the negative dimensions of patriarchy. Men are capable of great love of all kinds, yet they are also capable, wittingly and otherwise, of great cruelty and harm. When men behave violently or in a domineering (rather than dominant) way, 'patriarchy' is the name we could use to describe their acts. But our problem today seems more complicated. By dismantling patriarchy, via tote bags or otherwise, we have also collectively done away with all the *positive* dimensions of patriarchy as well: the protective father, the responsible man, the paternalistic attitude that exhibits care and compassion rather than simply places constraints on freedom. If anything, we have dismantled patriarchy in a rather extreme way, resulting in a horizontal, competitive society that suits consumer capitalism very well. Here there is no authority and power outside of that which this system and the state tells us there is. The state – whatever sex we attribute to it – Big Brother, the Nanny State – is no replacement for fatherly care of all kinds.

In 1963, the German psychoanalyst Alexander Mitscherlich wrote a book called *Society without the Father*. Mitscherlich suggests that a society without God, without any image of a father, becomes instead a *rivalrous* society. No longer struggling with Oedipal feelings, that is to say, no longer fighting with the father for freedom and power, the modern age becomes a world of sibling rivalry. We are less fathers and mothers, more brothers and sisters.[3] I think there is a profound truth in what Mitscherlich claims. We have lost respect and a relation to those older than us – at the same time, many of our elders have lost the desire to take responsibility for those younger than them. We have largely lost the benefits of generational wisdom and the shared knowledge that follows from experience. We are all competing for the same things and we have lost access to certain kinds of insights that belong to age and tradition. 'Equality', this great levelling, for all of its advantages, has come at some serious costs. To move towards a more graceful world, one that integrates history with the gains of modernity, that refuses to accept that sibling rivalry is our destiny, is required.

From Patriarchy to Male Privilege

There is a historical riddle at the heart of this conversation about patriarchy. If we accept that the patriarchy was overturned, or is still being overturned, in the name of the emancipation of women, what took so long? How did it happen? And before all this, why did women remain so historically passive? And not merely passive, we must say, but even complicit in their own apparent subordination. The feminist revaluation of history as one of male exploitation and female subservience that must be overcome is a relatively recent one, all things considered. As writer Alex Gendler argues, patriarchy can also be seen as a horror show for the vast majority of men too:

Contrary to both traditionalist conservative myth and popular feminist narrative, for most of history patriarchy was not a privilege one benefited from simply by being born male, but a brutal racket in which millions of men destroyed each other and the world around them for the benefit of a fortunate few.[4]

'Patriarchy' comes into focus, for feminist history, as a matter of enlightenment, of the awakening of women (and men) to the reality of our shared history. Women were prevented from reaching this feminist consciousness by being kept away from education, and by being kept in fear and ignorance through explicit and implicit coercion and violence.

But today there is equality, more or less – at least a debased, capitalist kind that forces men and women to work for a living. It is not equality from the standpoint of what humanity as a whole could be, perhaps, but there is a shift towards economic equality in the modern age. It is important to understand what progress has been made. It was made clear to all girls and women growing up in the 1990s, that we should not feel held back by our sex, that we could do and be anything. Being capable of doing anything and being encouraged to try non-traditional things is not, of course, the same as succeeding in them.

Patriarchy today is often understood alongside the idea of 'male privilege', another key term in today's attack on men. But how does privilege work? Arizona State University's 'Project Humanities' provides a 62-point list of male privileges based on a blog post by Julian Real entitled 'Unpacking the Male Privilege Jockstrap'.[5] Some of the points are the following: 'If I do the same task as a woman, and if the measurement is at all subjective, chances are people will think I did a better job'; 'If I have children and provide primary care for them, I'll be praised for extraordinary parenting if I'm even marginally competent', 'Among my male friends, I can speak with relative ease about the fact that I am horny without anyone attaching a negative term for what that is'; and, somewhat complicatedly, 'I have the privilege of being unaware of my male privilege'.

It may well be that men's work, parenting and sexual desire is sometimes regarded as more praiseworthy and notable than that of women – but who is judging here? We can all decide for ourselves what we value, beginning with our own thoughts and feelings. What does it matter to me what some imaginary other thinks? There is no free-floating thought out there, only the thoughts of individuals. If we decide individually or en masse to value child-care, no matter who does it, then that will be what we value (and we might find this value economically and socially). Rather than attacking 'male privilege', it would be better to raise up and cele-brate all positive behaviours: if mothers are currently overlooked or even demeaned, they should instead be respected and rewarded. After all, the future of humanity depends upon them.

Another problem with these kinds of descriptions of 'privil-ege', though, is that they presuppose a very specific kind of educated male behaviour. This discussion overlooks the vast dif-ferences in 'privilege' that obtain between men of different classes, and the very different circumstances that men and women might find themselves in. Listing 'privileges' in this way is per-haps ultimately just a way of making people feel guilty for things they needn't feel guilty for or can't help. This kind of stance is *itself* a privileged way of seeing the world, a kind of power, wielded over those susceptible to guilt.

It is certainly true, though, that some men sometimes act obnoxiously, particularly, in my experience (and not only mine), in swimming pools, where they somehow seem to enter a realm in which the moment their bodies are wet everyone else becomes invisible. As they plough up and down the lanes splashing and smacking the water, perhaps a kind of primal masculinity is tapped into, a kind of Tritonic force is unleashed.[6] If there is one criticism of male desire I would make in this book then it is this! *Swim kindly* . . . But we could equally say that everyone, regardless of the swim-gear they sport, is sometimes thoughtless.

In all seriousness, some men with power undoubtedly behave in ways that are unfair. Male behaviour has shifted radically over time. What man would today flirt with a female co-worker? Everyone has become extremely sensitized to 'power imbalances', while forgetting that there are many kinds of power, and that playfulness is all about these edges.

Do men, in any case, really hold all the power? It is on this question of where power lies that we should try to get clarity. Jean Baudrillard, in his 1979 book, *Seduction*, attempted to answer the question of what sexual power is. As he said: 'masculinity has always been haunted by [the] sudden reversibility within the feminine. Seduction and femininity are ineluctable as the reverse side of sex, meaning and power.'[7] There is no world of men, in other words, that is not shadowed by its opposite, feminine, force.

What Baudrillard suggests, ultimately, is that women have never lacked power: 'Feminism has never influenced me a great deal . . . It is truly one of the most advanced forms of *ressentiment*, which consists precisely in falling back on a demand for rights, "legitimate" and legal recrimination, whereas what is really at stake is symbolic power. And women have never lacked symbolic power.'[8]

Baudrillard's comments are, in one sense, infuriating. What on earth is 'symbolic' power in the face of material and legal power, we might ask? Shouldn't there be more women in Parliament, more female CEOs, more women in the legal profession? If the world continues to be run in the way it has been – as opposed to, for instance, being dismantled or radically altered somehow – why shouldn't women want more of a say, more representation, more inclusion in *this* world? It is fortunate, surely, that we live in an era in which women are no longer the 'property' of men. Feminism is undoubtedly one of the slowest and greatest revolutions in human history. In many senses, we are post-patriarchal, and justly so. So what can Baudrillard mean by 'symbolic power'? First of all, we have to admit that symbols are powerful. To play with images and signs, to create desire and longing, to be on the side of secrets and promises and riddles is indeed to possess a great game-playing power. To be 'equal' in difference is to recognize different registers of meaning.

Let's just say that all relationships are asymmetrical. Your boyfriend might be more sociable than you; you might have more money; he might be better-looking; you might have a better record collection, and so on. Power imbalances are clearly everywhere – some people are beautiful, some have money, or more time, are older, or have a job. The idea that romantic relationships should be some great leveller, a great restorer of the political justice so otherwise lacking in the world, is something of a fantasy. If we attempt to eliminate differences of 'power' between couples, the only person anyone can logically end up dating is oneself, and even then, if you got fired, or lost all your money, 'past you' couldn't go out with 'present you', as it would be unfair. In the face of competing and wildly uneven powers, there's nothing for it – we have to trust that people know what they're doing when they have a relationship with someone, and respect the fact that people find all kinds of different things to love in each other, including each other's flaws.

#MeToo in its 2017 iteration began in Hollywood but quickly spread, via the internet, to multiple institutions, everything from small business to schools to journalism, the army and the Church. #MeToo represented a 'changing of the guard', a re-ordering of the techniques of power, from the (no less horrific) old-school Hollywood sex-for-favours system to a highly mediated, technological world in which the internet (and occasionally the courts) could be used as a tool to shame men in particular who were perceived to overstep the mark. The ruling class might enter into mutually-assured-destruction pacts that involve horrifying rituals that bind them together, as Stanley Kubrick's *Eyes Wide Shut* suggests, but the ruling class itself has changed over time too. Our new overlords are masters, not only of social power, but of technological control.

'Power' has travelled in the West to the heart of the potentiality of technology itself. #MeToo was a trial of certain men, but also a reckoning with the limits of history itself – against an earlier world that didn't have everything recorded, so that proof of encounters didn't exist on tape, or in messages. The world we live in now operates as a kind of permanent recording device, and the internet is both the medium and the hidden heart of this totally surveilled world. It's increasingly obvious that anything anyone has written, sent or looked up online can be later used against them. Sexual encounters are still intimate at the level of flesh, but there is no doubt that they can be filmed, their existence noted on an app and so on. Will this ultimately make the world a safer place or a more dangerous one?

Who records the recorders? Who are the new custodians of our thoroughly tool-using modernity? Silicon Valley is not so very different in its after-work hours from any of the older industries. Money, power and men dominate. If these kinds of male monopolies always tend towards such behaviour, is it not better that we all understand this from the off? It would be better to educate both young men and young women, at home and at school, to point out that rich people want to have sex with good-looking people, and that if you would rather not be hurt, you need to stay away from such scenes. Where are the older people telling younger people that this is how the world works? If Silicon Valley is the apex of a certain culture, what does this tell us about the irresponsibility of our culture as a whole? To liberate desire so completely: this is the end-point of a certain human trajectory that might in fact be undoing itself.

It is not only the rich and powerful that behave badly, of course – we are all capable of harm, and we are all victims too. Taking responsibility for our own desire and character, whether we are curious, anxious, lustful, and so on, and weighing up situations before we enter them, as well as having a more forgiving attitude towards each other, could help avoid a childlike image of the world in which there are simply good guys and bad. Campaigns like #MeToo, for better or worse, make people think twice about what is and isn't appropriate. They also create an atmosphere of fear and anxiety over the smallest things. We live under constant surveillance. The twenty-first century will perhaps be a time of the recorded encounter, the documented consent, the algorithmic fuck. It will become harder to lie, but also harder to be carefree.

In tracking everything, in adjudicating and weighing up what counts as something that could later be used against someone, we have entered a truly horrible hall of mirrors. It is not surprising that many young men and women are choosing to opt out of this potential nightmare and settle down earlier, live traditionally and reasonably – exactly the kind of conservative or religious life that contemporary liberal culture set itself up in opposition to. To 'enjoy' on the terms of contemporary consumer capitalism and internet surveillance is a contradiction in terms. It is no wonder, then, that at the extremes we are seeing attacks on people, famous or otherwise, for 'power imbalances' in their relationships. If we water down terms such as 'abuse' to include any time anyone has been hurt, it will be safer simply to never engage with each other again. We will be consigned to a life lived 'safely' online, consuming the culture various platforms deem we should watch and talking to our 'friends' from behind virtual glass.

So, what, in the final analysis, of #MeToo? Was it a victory against patriarchy? These moments of collective reckoning and punishment might have served a cathartic, purifying function. Terrible things happened, and now we have entered into a collective kind of 'we don't do things like this any more' moment. But the internet proved to be a rather blunt tool, marking names indelibly with the stain of notoriety, even for minor transgressions that could have been handled in a different way – by talking to the person directly or, if that was too difficult, via mediation. The viral and often anonymous nature of the internet means that punishment-by-naming has an intense and uncontrollable quality, like a forest fire where the trees are someone's life and reputation. You might want in a moment of irritation to express your annoyance at a bad date or a thoughtless interaction, but it is impossible to predict where your words might end up, or the damage they might do.

Today's confusion over the nature of power sees only one side of the issue, which is power considered in its visible and rigid form. There are strands of feminism that concern the inclusion of women in typically male spheres and that see women's economic advancement as the ultimate victory for feminism, proof of its commitment to equality. However, this kind of liberal feminism has proved extremely compatible with the demands of capitalism in its indifference towards the sex of labourers, particular in factory and service economies. It is not at all clear that this situation truly liberates women from the shackles of the past. Winning a bad game is a Pyrrhic victory.

There is a kind of deadlock here, but also room for a more experimental approach. Mary Wollstonecraft in the eighteenth century proposed that if girls and women were naturally unsuitable for education then educating them would not hurt, but rather only prove the case against them. Her wager demonstrated something else – that girls and women could of course be educated, and they were, and continue to be. Today we have female participation in all kinds of previously male worlds, from paid labour to political power, although there have long been working women and queens. But the system being served here is arguably not one that recognizes anything beautiful or positive in sexual difference. For women to enter men's worlds or vice versa, in the name of a system of quantification and profit, is to work on behalf of something else entirely, not for each other, and not for the future. Capitalism is largely indifferent to sexual difference, except when it can profit from it. It is always indifferent to goodness.

Does it matter if women 'lean in', to quote Sheryl Sandberg, and get positions of power? These sorts of ambitions are only open to a small number of women by definition, and increasing the number of women in positions of power doesn't seem to change much, ultimately. Succeeding here perhaps only reinforces a particular system of domination and exploitation. But if some women want to play these games, why not? If they do, they must understand the stakes. As Camille Paglia writes,

> *Every* workplace is hostile for both women and men; testing, challenge, and potential sabotage are everywhere. Women must learn how to manoeuvre and negotiate for their own territory from the moment they arrive on the scene of any office or schoolroom.[9]

Men don't always play nice, but, then again, neither do women. Paglia makes the point that there should be no special allowances for women who wish to enter such 'territory'.

In any case, there are many things that are more interesting to do and think about than work (of course, we do not have a choice but to work, the vast majority of us). The specific model of employment that dominates today, where people travel for miles to spend hours doing something useless with people they don't necessarily like, is perhaps coming to a close, one way or another. We can imagine a different relation to work, where we all do what is necessary, and yet have enough to live on, and time to think and speak and care for one another. We are currently a long way from this other image – driving cars to car parks, eating tragic sandwiches, feeling stressed, having to use computers and wear depressing outfits.

Much labour has become indifferent to the sex of the person performing it, with some notable exceptions – for example, dangerous jobs and jobs that involve large amounts of strength are still dominated by men. In the US, for instance, men are significantly (more than ten times) more likely than women to be killed at work. The most dangerous jobs, according to the Bureau of Labor Statistics in 2019, were fishing and hunting, logging, piloting a small plane or helicopter, and roofing.[10] Men occupy 90 per cent of these jobs. Of the 144 people killed in workplace accidents in the UK in 2017–18, 96 per cent were men.[11] Whether we opt for an evolutionary explanation or a social one for why men take these kinds of employment – do women apply and are turned down? Are men encouraged to choose more dangerous work? – it is clear that there is no equality here (yet). Men's rights activists suggest that these are not the kinds of jobs where women would necessarily want parity. If these jobs are useful or even essential, it would make sense to value them more highly than jobs that do not involve such high levels of risk. A society that prioritizes safety over everything else forgets to have respect for those who take risks on its behalf.

To forget about sexual difference entails not seeing how the world is different for men and women. We run the risk of entering into a murky and confused era in which the body simply becomes another commodity/possession, the all-or-nothing surface of an imagistic age. The collapse of the ability to think about the difference between men and women, and male and female forms of power, is, I suggest, symptomatic of *a general collapse in the ability to think at all.*

It is not necessarily sexist or essentialist to say that men and women are different in interestingly compatible ways. Together we civilize each other. We curb each other's worst excesses. The graceful dance of men and women, regardless of their sexuality, is the stuff of culture. It makes us who we are, collectively.

The differences between men and women are important, even where there is also diversity within each sex. Aside from differences in muscle strength, speed, duration of fertility, and so on, women tend to be more agreeable than men, which is not of course to say that men are not or cannot be agreeable, sometimes more so than some women.[12] Nor does women's capacity to give birth, for example, entail that all women can (or should), only that every human that has ever given birth is female. No moral imperative follows from the statement of biological reality.

The sexual revolution was also supposed to usher in an age in which there was to be less shame about our bodies. Where women in particular could understand how their bodies worked, and feel more at ease with the reality of our physical existence. A virtual life pulls us back away from our nature, our human nature as well as our relation to the natural world, and it is no wonder that bodies start to seem like a source of sadness for many.

The modern world, despite its best efforts, cannot entirely flatten difference. It is not necessarily reactionary to point these differences out. On the contrary, it sets us back if we don't acknowledge material reality. By denying certain fundamental truths, we allow those with malign agendas to manipulate reality, and we allow ourselves to become confused puppets. It helps nothing and nobody to eliminate words such as 'woman' in favour of supposedly 'inclusive' terms such as 'womb-haver', 'menstruator' or 'birthing body'. Planned Parenthood and many other organizations have in recent years attempted in the name

of 'being kind' to people who don't identify as women to eliminate the use of this word in favour of mentioning biological
functions instead (men, it might be noted, are not however currently being renamed 'penis-havers' or 'testicle-bearers'). Many
feminists have taken issue with what seems like dehumanizing
language. As Meghan Murphy puts it in her discussion of Planned
Parenthood tweeting about 'menstruators', 'You see, the reason
patriarchy exists is because men decided they wanted control
over women's sexual and reproductive capacities. Not *people's*
sexual and reproductive capacities – *women's*.'[13]

Suggesting that there should be more respect for, let's say, the
reality (and beauty) of maternity does not, as disingenuous crit-
ics might suggest, mean 'reducing' women to wombs – not at
all. If women want to remain childfree and pursue a life of spiritual inquiry, live androgynously, or anything else, this is great,
but it is not for everyone. There have always been childless
women, though the social costs for remaining so were and are
often high – but none of us would be here without our mothers.
The deeply ambivalent feelings that female creativity, including
motherhood, induces in culture as a whole is worthy of collective discussion on the deepest levels. If some men resent women
for this, it should be openly discussed, not repressed and mutated
into weird envy.

Lundy Bancroft has worked with angry and controlling men
since 1987 and he is the author of a bestselling book on abuse
called *Why Does He Do That? Inside the Minds of Angry and Controlling Men*. Bancroft argues that abuse by men has less to do
with what men *feel* than what they already *think*. This implies
that abuse is less about flipping out than it is about certain pre-
existing mental states: if it is possible to change certain of these
assumptions, then abusive behaviour is less likely to occur in the
future. The implication here is important: if we want men to be
less harmful to each other, to women and to themselves, it must

be possible for minds to be changed. It is not women's responsibility to do this, of course, and perhaps they are often least well placed to do it. Men can instead help each other, and pass on ways in which they have come to understand that blaming women, individually and collectively, for their own negative feelings will only generate more suffering for all concerned.

For Bancroft, the male abuser believes he has a special status, that he deserves special treatment and, at the same time, believes he is exempt from accountability – that is, he imagines he is above criticism. Bancroft says that all of this is a matter of understanding what otherwise appears to be confusing and disorienting, not to mention harmful, behaviour. Male abuse of women is, in the first place, an extreme and immediate problem for the women being abused, but it is also a question for men as a whole, raising a number of questions about where *blame* is typically placed (often onto women as a whole, and onto particular women – 'she asked for it') as opposed to recognizing that the problem lies in the faulty and dangerous thought of harmful men. But it is important to remember that most men are not in fact violent, although all men (and women) are capable of violence. Whether we think we can change society or individuals first makes no difference to the main point here: if we can change people's assumptions, we can mitigate negative behaviour.

I'm personally convinced that if men could see themselves more often as *part* of a class of human beings called 'men', there would be much more success in getting men to help *other* men (i.e. other members of this class) to recognize, prevent and stop destructive and harmful behaviour of all kinds, whether inwardly directed or manifested in outward violence. Men could understand themselves far more effectively as part of a category of humanity united by their shared sex. Women are often treated in this way, in fact, as first and foremost bearers of their sex, *before* they are understood to be individuals or responsible primarily for themselves. 'Women' are often spoken about as if an individual woman stands in for all women (it often feels like this, in any case). Many men are loath to accept the possibility of understanding themselves in this way, and it's true that women often feel it's unfair when men seek to tar them all with the same brush or to see in a particular woman their sex as a whole. But perhaps if men could see each other in a similar way, and take responsibility for other men, *as men*, then a lot of damage could be avoided and mitigated: 'Your behaviour is making the rest of us look bad . . . let me help you sort it out.'

Far from possessing great power, men are frequently trapped in systems of other men's making. To be entranced by worldly goods and to be overly concerned with the recognition of other people, for example, is to be highly dependent on the world in its basest sense. These attitudes do not demonstrate a positive relation to power and control. No doubt there are individual men who exploit their status, one way or another, and for these cruelties they should be punished *by their fellow men above all*, who suffer by association with the actions of bad men. This is, again, not a question of blaming all men for the sins committed by a few, but of all men taking responsibility for all others – for guiding them and helping them.

Everywhere, generalizations abound. When a woman posts something accompanied by the hashtag #KillAllMen on Twitter we could say that she is tapping into a legitimate sense of grievance against particular men who may have personally hurt or abused her or other women. She is, in other words, railing against 'patriarchy'. But we could equally find such a statement abhorrent. The hashtag would be unlikely to be tolerated if the word 'men' were swapped out for any other category of humanity, including 'women'. Even if it remains a general sideswipe against men, is there anything defensible about it? As psychology professor Geoffrey Miller puts it: 'Funny how many of the same people who think that #KillAllMen is a light-hearted joke also feel outraged if anyone mentions the stats that men suffer higher rates of accidents, homicides, suicides, and all-cause mortality than women, throughout life.'[14] The spectre of a zero-sum suffering game appears on the horizon. Making men suffer for the suffering of women will not end violence.

Most perpetrators and victims of murder worldwide are male: 78.7 per cent according to the UN, and in 193 of the 202 countries or regions listed, males were more likely to be killed than females.[15]

Men, when they commit violence, generally do damage to other men and to themselves. They also, of course, hurt women, though less often than they hurt other men. Women's risks increase when they are in an intimate relationship with a man or male family member. The UN estimates that of women who were the victims of murder globally in 2012, almost half were killed by intimate partners or family members, compared to less than 6 per cent of men killed in the same year.[16] It is not that women are incapable of or never commit violence against themselves, each other, or men – they sometimes do – but it's rarer.

So #KillAllMen is, on one level, ironic hyperbole on the part of the women using it – possible to say because it so rarely happens. Some uses of the tag are humorous: 'When your office thermostat is controlled by a MAN even here in Hawai'i we are forced to use space heaters. #killallmen.'[17]

Some men, such as *Vox* magazine founder Ezra Klein, defended the sentiment:

A few years ago, it became popular on feminist Twitter to tweet about the awful effects of patriarchal culture and attach the line #KillAllMen. This became popular enough that a bunch of people I know and hang out with and even love began using it in casual conversation.

And you know what? I didn't like it. It made me feel defensive. It still makes me feel defensive. I'm a man, and I recoil hearing people I care about say all men should be killed.

But I also knew *that wasn't what they were saying.* They didn't want me put to death. They didn't want any men put to death. They didn't hate me, and they didn't hate men. '#KillAllMen' was another way of saying 'it would be nice if the world sucked less for women'. It was an expression of frustration with pervasive sexism. I didn't enjoy the way they said it, but that didn't mean I had to pretend I couldn't figure out what they meant. And if I had any questions, I could, you know, *ask*, and actually listen to the answer.[18]

Klein's uneasy justification for the hashtag is symptomatic of a certain kind of contemporary impasse between men and women – 'She can't really mean it . . . can she?' What, though, if it were *not* a plea for 'less sucking' for women, whatever *that* might mean, but a genuine androcidal call to arms? I don't for one second think that the women (and few men) using the #KillAllMen hashtag *really* want to or would kill men, given the chance, let alone 'all' of them, but there is nevertheless a weird bloodthirstiness beneath the clearly hyperbolic phrase, however ironic its users might say it is. Reminiscent of the undecidable tone of Valerie Solanas's 1967 'SCUM Manifesto' – the call 'to civic-minded, responsible, thrill-seeking females' to 'overthrow the government, eliminate the money system, institute complete automation and destroy the male sex'[19] – the hashtag exists in a kind of no-man's-land of meaning.

Perhaps, we could say with some justice, women have had enough of playing the peacemaker, of being nice. Is the hashtag then a response to a structural question – the unequal distribution of power and money? Or to the asymmetrical violence men mete out to women (though far more to each other)?

Apart from war, male-on-male violence is an omnipresent threat and worry for men, though for some more than others; and for some and in some places it is an endlessly acute one. What can women say about the violence men inflict on each other? Patriarchy, if we accept that this term refers to something real, *absolutely hurts men too*.

We're accustomed to thinking of violence as an action committed by individuals against others, but there is a deeper, more historical and even more metaphysical question regarding the nature of violence, or indeed the violence of nature. As animals, human beings are apex predators, which is to say that through a combination of brute force and intelligence we have managed to dominate the planet. We are partial to war, revolution and aggression; to the unleashing of various destructive instincts at times. It takes an immense amount of training, conditioning and time to 'civilize' humanity.

Our cities, our libraries, our art galleries, and indeed the mainly peaceful and diplomatic negotiations between the sexes, are the positive outcome of a repressed and sublimated way of living together. Violence belongs to the species itself, and beyond the species, to a cruel and indifferent nature, rather than being merely the domain of the male portion of humanity.

It is important for men and women to understand and indeed confront some unpalatable truths, not least because if we understand our own role in rivalry, competition, violence and war, we can help in the reimagining of a world in which these things are known as possibilities for the future of humanity as a whole. Rather than imagining that women are somehow always on the side of peace, or that 'Lehman Sisters', as Christine Lagarde, head of the IMF suggests,[20] would have somehow brought about a kinder capitalism, we would all do better to accept and integrate our own aggressive instincts, the better to live with them more peaceably. They always remain beneath, buried to some extent by taming and normalizing forces, only to reappear again on another level. We are animals with a thin coating of poetry.

Our age often promotes, inculcates and celebrates infantilism and complaint. Recently psychologists have identified a 'novel personality trait' to which they have given the name the 'tendency for interpersonal victimhood'. They describe this trait in the following way: 'an enduring feeling that the self is a victim across different kinds of interpersonal relationships'.[21] The authors note that

> Social life is replete with situations that are open to interpretation. We wait for people who are late for meetings, are surprised by people who interrupt us when we speak, and are annoyed when co-workers tackle our initiatives. While some people overcome such incidents with relative ease, and view them as an unpleasant but an unavoidable part of social life, others tend to be preoccupied with having been hurt long after the event has ended; they consider themselves to have been victims of others' malevolent actions . . . People who have a higher tendency for interpersonal victimhood feel victimized more often, more intensely, and for longer durations in interpersonal relations than do those who have a lower such tendency.[22]

While the researchers here are identifying a pathology, it does not seem too far-fetched to be concerned with the way in which human beings are swayed en masse by cultural trends. Perhaps we will move from the age of the victim to the age of responsibility once more – although this can only happen if those cut out of the traditional markers of adulthood are allowed to grow up. And this is, above all, an economic question. Who today can afford to be an adult? Nevertheless, both men and women have a duty to resist this easy escape into childishness, which in turn does a disservice to actual children who need our adult protection and care.

★

On 3 April 2018, Nasim Aghdam, a 38-year-old animal rights activist, brought a Smith & Wesson 9mm calibre semi-automatic pistol to the San Bruno headquarters of YouTube. She was aggrieved with the company for allegedly stifling traffic and suppressing her videos on the site. She once wrote, 'There is no free speech in the real world and you will be suppressed for telling the truth that is not supported by the system.' Aghdam thought she had discovered a fundamental injustice in the suppression of her speech. YouTube, she said, 'censor and suppress people who speak the truth and are not good for the financial, political gains of the system and big businesses'.

Aghdam, who hated technology, nevertheless felt compelled to spread her message online in a series of bizarre videos that combined gymnastic routines with pro-animal and pro-vegan rhetoric. When that didn't work, and she felt her message was being censored, she took her weapon to a corporation and shot three random people, and then herself. The FBI, in a study of Active Shooter Incidents in the US between 2000 and 2013, stated that out of the 160 incidents they tracked, only six were committed by women. Aghdam was, however, at least statistically on target by shooting up a commercial building and turning the gun on herself, as 45 per cent of shootings analysed by the FBI took place in places of business or work and around 40 per cent also ended in suicide.

What can Aghdam's act tell us? About the contemporary relationship between gender and the desire for economic and social recognition, say? About the vexed question of violence as it relates to what it means to be a man or a woman today?

Aghdam's sympathy for animals was no doubt genuine. She is quoted in an old news report as saying 'animal rights equal human rights' while standing outside a military base protesting the use of pigs in military trauma training. But she also felt that her *human* rights were violated as a consequence of YouTube's alleged suppression of her videos. Aghdam's acting out was possibly a last-ditch attempt to both promote her cause and achieve a certain kind of recognition, albeit a horrific, terminal one.

There is no longer any public or dominant channel of image dissemination, only competing platforms that may or may not remain relatively insular, even as some have millions upon millions of viewers. In his 2003 novel, *Millennium People*, J. G. Ballard envisaged a world where the middle class would rise up, tired of their comfort, complacency and culture. In interviews, he imagined members of the middle class attacking art-house cinemas and museums. But what we have today is even more unhinged in every sense – attacks on corporations which are themselves not singular sites like art galleries, but rather bearers of their corporate identity, which exists everywhere and nowhere in the ether, taking over all the words for the atmosphere as we used to know it – the cloud, sky, birdsong – the internet is the universe. All of its names are stolen from the cosmos, as if trying to usurp nature.

The internet encourages us all, men and women alike, to make icons of our bodies, to push for a kind of infinite and impossible recognition. There are not enough eyes and not enough time to see every image, even the ones we generate ourselves. If a video plays online and no one is around to see it, does it even exist? Merely knowing that everything you can possibly imagine – from the utterly macabre, vile, senseless, illegal and highly disturbing to the cute, cheering and friendly – exists on video is, somehow, to have seen them. We have become browsers, video players, pianolas trying to read too many rolls at once. But we are the ones being played.

Since June 2018, Netflix employees are apparently banned from looking at each other for more than five seconds, an edict which Netflix neither confirms nor denies.[23] If the gaze today is a form of violence, and language potentially always a miscommunication open to prosecution, legal or otherwise, then we will inevitably end up in multiple forms of segregation, imposed or chosen for reasons of self-preservation. This is a far cry from Deneuve *et al.*'s desire to defend, against the logic of #MeToo, 'this freedom to bother in ways other than by closing ourselves off'.

We run the risk, if not of violent acting-out, of at least acting hastily, of generating more hatred and ire than we perhaps even intended. We are all potentially violent, physically, mentally, emotionally. We all cause harm. We can nevertheless learn how to live together amid the confusion and ruins of modernity. How can we do this while recognizing the reality of damage and suffering? There is damage and there is perpetuating damage; and punishing someone is itself an act of aggression. Social mechanisms for preventing the escalation of violence exist for a good reason, but we can do this individually and interpersonally too. In fact, we must.

Ask yourself, if you have been hurt by someone – as we all have – can you deal with it without reaching for revenge? If you cannot, what will be gained by vengeance? Have you yourself done something wrong, even something wrong in a similar way? Wouldn't you want also to be forgiven? To live in an unforgiving society is to live in fear. None of these deep anthropological, philosophical and religious questions have disappeared just because we can put off social reality by listlessly eating crisps while pretending to be modern.

Patriarchy and Virility

How to be good? If virility or goodness are discussed at all today it is invariably in a snide or ironic way. To call a man 'virile' today is to limit the word to its sexual sense alone. Virility, though, has a far more complex and more moral history than we might imagine, and one that ties men to goodness in an interesting way.

Etymologically, we get the word 'virtue' from *vir*, an ancient term across several languages that means, above all, 'man'. Virility is thus not simply a question of what one does with one's 'manhood' or how often one does it. For the Ancient Greeks, to be a man was not to display one's sexual prowess, nor was it to enact brute force or to be aggressive in any way. It was instead a question of behaviour of the noblest and highest kinds. Above all, to be virile was to be self-possessed and to take care of oneself, the better to support others. It was something, in fact, women too could be occasionally – for example, Antigone when she courageously buries her brother against the wishes of the state.

To stress the moral and political dimension of virility is not to obscure the knee-jerk associations we have today in relation to this term. Certainly, for the Greeks, virility was *also* a question of physical dexterity, but this was an image of physical self-possession that is a long way from today's obsession with outward appearance, which is separated from inner grace. For the Greeks, the connection between physical beauty and moral qualities was much closer.

Ideas of virtue and beauty are today somewhat tarnished, if not entirely absent. It would be nevertheless perhaps possible to imagine a world where physical and moral bearing were brought closer together again. Looking after one's own health, both mental and physical, allows everyone to be better placed to encourage others to be more active, and less melancholic. Well-being is collective, and does not only relate to mere vanity, but rather to well-rounded characters and culture. 'Beauty' today is a term primarily reserved and deployed in relation to, and sometimes against, women. The encouragement of virtue among men might also involve the generation of a new conception of male beauty. To reopen the question of the beauty of all is simultaneously to pose the question of what it might mean to live together more harmoniously.

There are some men today in possession of what the Greeks valued above all, that is to say courage, and there are men who think in terms of the collective good, not in order to subsume themselves under some anonymous image of humanity, but rather the better to encourage goodness in all. For men, to be virtuous is not only to know when to deploy strength and understanding, but also, consequently, to have an attitude of general concern for everyone. The main way to encourage virtue in men for the benefit of all would be not only to encourage relationships of male mentorship and education but also to celebrate the existence and benefits of male friendship as they exist today. Male friendship, that is to say, the desire of men to enjoy each other's company, is frequently the subject of jibes from both men and women. Just as being 'virile' is often reduced to an erection, male friendship is often dismissed as being somehow silly or borderline homosexual.[24]

But friendship between men exists, it is real, and can encourage virtue. To reduce everything to sex – the threat or fear or desire for sex – is to radically narrow the other dimensions of relating within and between the sexes. There is friendship without sex, playfulness without threat and affection without fear, between men and men, and between men and women.

A more honest discussion of different kinds of affection has been eclipsed by a desire for identity. We live in the aftermath of the sexual revolution, and our culture is awash in pornography and lusts of all kinds. Religious ideas about sex are more or less completely overturned, although we must also note that some young people have reverted back to a more 'traditionalist' way of thinking. As Pepin and Cotter put it in their recent research on 'traditionalism':

After becoming more egalitarian for almost twenty years, high school seniors' thinking about a husband's authority and divisions of labor at home has since become substantially more traditional. In 1976, when they were asked whether 'it is usually better for everyone involved if the man is the achiever outside the home and the woman takes care of the home and family', fewer than 30 percent of high school seniors disagreed. By 1994, disagreement with the claim that the male breadwinner–female homemaker family is the best household arrangement had almost doubled, rising to 58 percent. By 2014, however, it had *fallen back* to 42 percent—a decline of 16 percentage points since its peak in 1994. In 1976, a majority of high school seniors (59 percent) disagreed with the statement that 'the husband should make all the important decisions in the family'. This rose to 71 percent by 1994 but fell back to 63 percent by 2014.[25]

For better or worse, the sexually liberated, egalitarian moment may have peaked. What does this mean for sex in the future? If sex is something to do with pleasure, and our 'identity' is something to do with our sexual being, then we are all reduced to walking declarations of desire. We live in an age in which the fusion of a certain kind of consumerism is perfectly compatible with the harnessing of this model of desire, which is to say, desire becomes nothing other than *consumption*.

We might feel on some level a deep sense of freedom and gratitude for this 'liberation': no longer are we tethered to our actions in the same way as our ancestors were. This freedom, however, the freedom to 'screw around' is also a freedom to screw up. The 'sexual utopia' promised by sexual liberation has arguably hit its limits: we are now perhaps in whatever comes after: Thermidor? As Louise Perry puts it: 'Our grandmothers were called sluts if they wanted anything other than missionary. Today's young women risk being called frigid if they say no to the porn-soaked fantasies presented to them as freedom.'[26]

Baudrillard, once again, captures our predicament:

> If I were asked to characterize the present state of affairs, I would describe it as 'after the orgy'. The orgy in question was the moment when modernity exploded on us, the moment of liberation in every sphere. Political liberation, sexual liberation, liberation of the forces of production, liberation of the forces of destruction, women's liberation, children's liberation, liberation of unconscious drives, liberation of art . . . This was a total orgy – an orgy of the real, the rational, the sexual, of criticism as of anti-criticism, of development as a crisis of development . . . Now everything has been liberated, the chips are down, and we find ourselves faced collectively with the big question: WHAT DO WE DO NOW THAT THE ORGY IS OVER?[27]

After the orgy, after the party, we survey the wreckage: what do we see? A lot of confusion, a lot of blame, and a desire for someone to take responsibility.

We have to go back to old truths in a new way. Here we are on difficult territory. If we want to say that men and women are different in important ways, what follows from these assertions of difference? Reading some parts of the manosphere, particularly those relating to dating, it is necessary to be prepared to encounter some harsh ways of seeing the world. One word you'll encounter a lot in the way men write online about dating is 'hypergamy', the idea that women are always looking for the 'best' man. This idea, although initially perhaps shocking, nonetheless offers some useful insight. Paul Elam, prominent Men's Rights Activist and founder of the website 'A Voice for Men' puts it like this:

Hypergamy means marrying up; marrying into a higher social or financial class. It's an obscure word considering that it is the objective of about 98% of women in this society who want to marry. Its counterpart word, hypogamy, describes women who marry down, beneath their means. All three of them.[28]

Online, 'hypergamy' generally refers to heterosexual women who seek to maximize the value of their mating potential by consistently pursuing, consciously or otherwise, the highest-status men that they can acquire sexually. If (unlike the classic romantic fantasy) such a prince won't marry her after she's slept with him, she'll look for a boring accountant instead to support her and her children.

I think that even though this is a pretty unpleasant way of seeing the world, it is better that women know this is the way some men see them. One particularly succinct way of putting it is 'alpha fucks, beta bucks', i.e. high-status men impregnate women, and other men pay for the women and children. I must admit I find this way of seeing things brutal, and I wonder what effect it has on the young men who accept this idea. To imagine that women are merely 'hypergamous' is to ascribe to them a deeply calculating tendency, conscious or otherwise. I've personally never met a woman who has explicitly expressed 'hypergamous' views, which is not to say, of course, that therefore they do not exist. Women naturally want the best for themselves and their children.

We are animals, and are driven in part by biological forces. There is a limit to what can be socially 'improved' in us through culture and education, especially if these things are not themselves committed to virtue, but only utility. Perhaps if we took this fact seriously it might have some interesting positive effects: men would look to improve themselves, mentally and physically, as many already do; we would all understand that sex is perhaps more serious than we sometimes think it is – it does, after all, create bonds even when it is 'casual'. 'Don't catch feelings' is a phrase used by people who choose to have casual sex via hook-up apps, because the worst thing in the world would of course be to start to care about someone you're having meaningless sex with.

But are there really 'alpha' and 'beta' men and women, as the manosphere would have it? Would the most 'alpha' man be the strongest? Many extremely strong men can be found in prison, which hardly indicates that being hyper-masculine did them any favours. Is the highest-status man in our culture a rich man? Many of these men are physically weak, yet they appear 'alpha' in other ways. Are we just chimpanzees with pretensions? When we love someone, we do so perhaps for many reasons, but character surely features strongly in our feeling. This love is obviously not first and foremost about whether they could beat another animal to death in a fight, but rather a question of the unique nature of the other person.

By any definition there can only be a few 'alpha' men, yet young girls are encouraged to think of themselves as princesses to an alarming degree, which seems to demand the necessary existence of multiple princes. Yet princes are, of necessity, rare: most men will live and die as commoners in the game of love and war and possess very little of the spoils of either. The princess narrative is usually presented as a harmless piece of fun – dress-up, prettiness, pink and frills with a wand and tiara – but its implications are narrow: spoil me, rescue me, woo me. In my lifetime I think we have seen a series of regressions in relation to possibilities for expression and roles for both boys and girls, men and women: for all the contemporary exploration of 'gender diversity', the gendered roles themselves (boys must be tough and like 'boy things'; girls must be delicate and like 'girl things') have been relentlessly pushed by companies and culture alike through toys and TV shows. How much better it is to live freely, trying to be as a good as you can be as the particular man or woman you happen to be, and to learn that there is no one perfect way to do this.

But in our rush today to condemn patriarchy and virility as such we are in danger of throwing the baby boy out with the bathwater, neglecting the fact that men will *continue* to exist in the world. Men are not going anywhere. Nor are women, for that matter. We are unlikely to make it back to Mars or Venus in our lifetimes, whatever Elon Musk might be planning. We are in a particularly volatile time – the recent grand historical staging of resentment against men follows centuries of women being positioned alternately as witches or doll-like things. History proceeds by its darker side, and monsters are eventually brought to light, slaughtered and then buried again, only to re-emerge once more, like zombies.

From the moment someone says, 'It's a boy!', certain expectations are cultivated. Some of these expectations might be felt negatively, of course: a sensitive boy might recoil from the demand that he 'act tough' and avoid crying, a gentle man might feel deep pain at the violence some members of his sex inflict on others. If we have today reached a certain uneasy kind of equality between men and women, there remain some residual questions regarding social life. Men are not exactly coterminous with masculinity, but there are definitely better and worse ways of being a man. If 'patriarchy' is the name, ultimately, for a set of confusions, 'masculinity' too functions these days more to obscure and condemn than to elucidate.

3.   Is Masculinity the Problem?

Respect the cock! And tame the cunt! Tame it!

Frank T. J. Mackey, pick-up artist, played by Tom Cruise
in *Magnolia* (1999, dir. Paul Thomas Anderson)

However we feel about masculinity – whether we think that all forms are 'bad', or that some kinds are positive and should be encouraged – we must discuss it. Our image of masculinity is conditioned by history, but it is also reflective of and reflected in contemporary and shifting social expectations that come from all sides. Today, for example, parents tend no longer to leave baby boys on roofs or bathe them in wine to see if they are tough enough to survive, as the Spartans did. To argue that a particular kind of masculinity follows from nature is potentially tricky, yet dispensing with the link between nature and culture altogether also generates new and potentially worse ideas; for example, that we can dispense with our bodies completely. As Philosopher Nick Bostrom, writing about transhumanism, puts it:

> It may . . . be possible to upload a human mind to a computer, by replicating *in silico* the detailed computational processes that would normally take place in a particular human brain. Being an upload would have many potential advantages, such as the ability to make back-up copies of oneself (favorably impacting on one's life-expectancy) and the ability to transmit oneself as information at the speed of light.[1]

For the time being, however, we remain sexed. We are still animals, albeit awkward ones. We created a shared reality on the basis of the world we have all been given. The existence of language and culture does not permit the individual untethering of our being or desire from our genetics or our sex: we are all in this together, and sometimes our desires are opposed. But men and women are not fundamentally mortal enemies.

There is always, we are supposed to say, a crisis of masculinity. It is tempting, in fact, to say that masculinity *is* crisis, in the same way that the banner for the 2011 London Occupy movement stated that 'Capitalism *Is* Crisis'. For some, the crisis is that men are not masculine enough. For others, the problem is masculinity as such. As one of Britain's foremost observers of men, artist Grayson Perry, puts it:

> It is a newsroom cliché that masculinity is always somehow 'in crisis', under threat from pollutants such as shifting gender roles, but to me many aspects of masculinity seem such a blight on society that to say it is 'in crisis' is like saying racism was 'in crisis' in civil-rights-era America. Masculinity needs to change.[2]

Perry suggests that he sometimes thinks that 'all the world's problems can be boiled down to one thing: the behaviour of people with a Y chromosome.'[3] But masculinity and men are not to blame for *all* the world's woes. This statement is, however, typical of current thinking about masculinity and about men. *Men are to blame*. Masculinity is rotten to the core and must be thrown away, and men must accept that they are at fault. On the other hand, there seems something almost embarrassing about wanting to be more masculine, as if having to work for it undermines something about its very nature.

But think for a moment of a world *without* masculinity (or femininity) of any kind, in which men and women could enjoy anything they liked, have multiple interests, wear whatever they felt like and love whoever they wanted. Biological sex would be noted for medical and reproductive purposes, but otherwise would be of little concern in day-to-day life. Character would be paramount: we would like people primarily for who they are, not what they are.

This is not a new idea: many feminists have been imagining this world – one in which sex-role stereotypes were abolished – for a long time. This kind of social freedom inevitably clashes with the image of a divided human nature pushed by some men's rights activists, where, as we have seen, women are always secretly vying for the 'best man', and the world is viewed as set against men and in favour of women. But it also clashes with some of our deepest intuitions about sexual difference: that men and women are different, even if, in many situations, these differences don't or shouldn't matter.

So, there's a social question: Are there too many female role models, for example, and not enough male ones for young men to emulate? Boys do struggle, and it would be unjust to suggest that they do not. Much ink has been spilled and many hands wrung over the fate of boys in the current education system, for example. Why do boys often now do so much worse than girls? Is male 'bad behaviour' at school somehow expected or encouraged? It must be possible to imagine and encourage positive kinds of masculinity where boys and men feel the kind of pride that would encourage self-respect and the respect and love of their peers.

Actor Robert Webb, in his memoir, *How Not to Be a Boy*, comes to similar conclusions, stating that 'Men will struggle to treat women as equals if we haven't learned to look after ourselves; to recognize our feelings and take responsibility for our actions. We should remember what we knew all along: that we are allowed to be fully human, fully compassionate, fully alive in the moment and fully committed to friendship and love.'[4]

Men and masculinity are not quite the same thing, of course, and if the latter is somehow superimposed upon the former, we must say that it is not exactly obvious what it means to be a man today, or what a masculine, or non-masculine, man might be. Nevertheless, certain things should be clear from the outset, most importantly: *to be a man is not in itself a bad thing.*

Masculinity is also not necessarily 'toxic' or harmful or violent or oppressive. To be a man today is, in great part, and at the risk of sounding dramatic, to *suffer* (this is *not* to suggest that women don't suffer: of course they do, only their suffering takes different forms and is not the primary subject here). Suicide is the biggest killer of men under forty-five and 75 per cent of suicides are male.[5] In 2017, 4,382 men took their own lives in the UK.[6] Men are 67 per cent more likely to die of cancer than women when sex-specific forms of the disease are excluded.[7] They are more likely to be homeless (71 per cent).[8] Nine out of ten people who die during or after police custody are men.[9] Figures from the UK Home Office Homicide Index for the year ending March 2017 show that 74 per cent of murder victims were male and 26 per cent were female.[10] Men die younger. Men are often treated poorly when it comes to gaining access to their children, a source of much anger. Controversial custody rights group Fathers4Justice suggests that 'There is more legislation protecting animals than there is protecting fathers.'[11]

One of the difficult aspects of discussing male and female grievances is the way in which men and women are so often pitted against one another. Even the framing of the statistics above carries the implication that if it is better (or worse) for one sex, then things are better (or worse) for the other. But this is a highly limited way of seeing the world. It encourages resentment of both individuals and groups and is implicitly predicated on the idea that the relationship between men and women is a zero-sum game, in which there is somehow a finite amount of health or love or care or even violence to go around, and that the distribution will always be unfair in one direction or the other.

It would not be better if women died of cancer more often or suffered *more* violence in order to 'balance out' the misery. Men may need to be encouraged to go to the doctor more often, in order to get an earlier diagnosis. It would be better to cure cancer completely and to eliminate, to the extent to which it is possible, the violence suffered by both men and women.

Let me be clear again: the vast majority of violence is perpetrated by men: in the year ending March 2018, nine times more women and men were killed by their male partner or ex-partner in England and Wales,[12] and as N. Quentin Woolf puts it,

> Men commit more violent crime than women, by a mile. Around 85–90 per cent of convicted murderers are men, a majority of the reported domestic abusers and pretty much all of those committing sexual attacks. However – and this is the part that gets overlooked – almost twice as many men than women are the victims of violence.[13]

Men hurt and get hurt often: 'the greatest sufferers from men's violence are other men' writes Rosalind Miles.[14] We should also note that more attention has been paid in recent years to the suffering of men in domestic violence incidents. The ManKind Initiative, the first charity set up to support male victims of domestic abuse, was established in 2001. They report that, as of March 2018

> 4.3% of men and 7.5% of women stated that they have experienced domestic abuse in 2016/17, equivalent to an estimated 713,000 male victims and 1.2 million female victims. For every three victims of domestic abuse, two will be female, one will be male. The difference between the prevalence of domestic abuse for men and women is at its lowest since the year ending March 2005.[15]

The zero-sum-game idea (where if one party benefits the other must lose) arguably dominates our social thinking in general, though perhaps nowhere more so than in the realm of dating and sex between men and women. However, the idea that no one gains something without someone else losing it is an assumption that profoundly hinders the way we think about how we might relate to one another *in general*. Ultimately, a more compassionate and understanding attitude to the suffering of both sexes, in all its complexity and difference at the individual and group level, is desirable.

This might mean coming to terms with the rather paradoxical idea that men and women are both different and equal at the same time. We are sometimes pushed by our culture to imagine that men and women are somehow unable to communicate with one another properly (the 'Men are from Mars' hypothesis) and that decoding the opposite sex is a mystery akin to poring over ancient languages whose meaning has been lost. Yet men and women are not quite the same, either biologically or in terms of the way in which expectations and social existence are imposed and lived, explicitly and implicitly. To repeat again, we cannot *exactly* know what life is like for the opposite sex, though we can try to sympathetically and humorously imagine it.

There are of course many, many texts and arguments circulating that attempt to either maximize or minimize the difference between men and women on a variety of different grounds, some scientific, some more vividly ideological: 'brain sex', hormonal differences, hardwired psychological difference, evolutionary psychology, sexual selection or a combination of all of these are often invoked to explain sex differences or disparities. Cordelia Fine, for instance, writes:

The neuroscientific discoveries we read about in magazines, newspaper articles, books and sometimes even journals tell a tale of two brains – essentially different – that create timeless and immutable psychological differences between the sexes. It's a compelling story that offers a neat, satisfying explanation, and justification of the gender status quo.[16]

Fine argues that the attempt to seek out differences has a long and largely ignoble history, which led to women being denied access to education and to texts of all kinds, as well as employment and many other social roles. We are absolutely flooded today and historically with 'gender', that is to say, for the purposes of the definition under investigation here, the stereotypes and roles imposed upon both sexes. As Fine puts it: 'When gender is salient in the environment, or we categorize someone as male or female, gender stereotypes are automatically primed.'[17]

What would a world in which people could do and be whoever they wanted without fear of disapproval look like? Is it possible to imagine a world beyond or after gender? We seem to live on the cusp of a huge range of possible technological transformations of the human, and we ourselves are profoundly implicated and changed by technology. Yet we still, for the time being, *have bodies*, beyond which we cannot think, even if we alter them quite radically. I'm not even really sure we can change them, or our nature, that much in the end, despite our love of the future. Everybody *is a body*, and likely just the one. It is strange that this seems like a radical thing to say.

Spending our lives feeling bad about our bodies is extremely miserable, and there is no doubt we live in a culture in which both male and female bodies are judged negatively at different times and for different reasons. It is no surprise, perhaps, in understanding contemporary masculinity, that fitness and working out have become such dominant features of the masculinist landscape – a way of life.

In a 2018 essay entitled 'What Is It Like to Be a Man?', American writer and tutor Phil Christman writes:

> As real as I know male privilege to be – and if I forget it for a moment, I have the newspapers to remind me – it is surreal to find maleness, an aspect of my life that I associate mainly with chosen discomfort, equated now, by so many people, with bovine self-complacency.[18]

In his thoughtful, reflective piece, Christman determines that his attitude to his own masculinity is one of a 'perverse' relation to discomfort, of deliberately choosing the hard or unpleasant option, as well as a desire to look after others:

> When I try to nail down what masculinity is – what imperative gives rise to all this pain seeking and stoicism, this showboating asceticism and loud silence – I come back to this: Masculinity is an *abstract rage to protect*.[19]

This is quite a beautiful and revealing suggestion: '*an abstract rage to protect*'! To link anger and care in the same breath – here we do seem close to the truth of something, however thwarted this 'rage to protect' might be in actuality. While Christman suggests that 'protectors always fail', he nevertheless uncovers a fracturing thought: what happens when men cannot protect? Today we have 'neutral' states that are supposed to protect us equally: we do not call on men specifically to do the work of protecting, even if men still dominate those jobs that require often dangerous actions to save others (the services, the armed forces, much physical labour).

To be in a heterosexual relationship as a woman is to understand, perhaps, something of the male desire to protect, and to be protected. However tough you feel, however independent you might be, when it comes down to it, you would like a man to be able to stand up for you, physically at least. You make a deal: I am with you so you will protect me from other men, and even perhaps, sometimes, from myself. Not all women might feel like this, it is true, but I can't help but recognize this desire at least partly in myself. Violence is not as far away from care as we might like to imagine. The capacity to protect is also to be in possession of the means of enacting that protection, otherwise care has no ground. Every social encounter between men is potentially a fistfight, Christman writes. Men are wary of one another. Men are inclined to avoid each other's eyes.

For Christman, to be a man is to undertake

> the activities that stem from a fear that simple usefulness is not enough: that one must train and prepare for eventualities one has no reason to anticipate, must keep one's dwelling and grooming spartan in case of emergencies, must undertake defensive projects that have no connection to the actual day-to-day flourishing of the people one loves.[20]

What if we could connect back up this almost comically stoical, ascetic masculinity to the 'day-to-day flourishing' of others? Masculinity does not have to become redundant, then, but rather it can be held always in reserve, and can be compatible with the flourishing of others, as Christman notes. We shouldn't simply refuse the idea that men can and should be protective and look after those around them, even while we want freedom and joy for all. For men to opt out of all positive ideas of masculinity is for them to accept the incredibly debased terms of a world that encourages an absence of thought and feeling towards others. To care is also to be strong, to be brave.

If masculinity was simply reducible to a series of negative attributes, there would be no reason why anybody would want men around, let alone want to *be* one. Second-wave feminists pointed out that gender roles imposed on boys and girls were often highly restrictive and destructive to both sexes. Their solution was *not* to deny the reality of sexual dimorphism but rather to work to positively expand the categories of gender expression so that, for example, girls who enjoyed pursuits typically associated with boys were still girls, and similarly boys who enjoyed supposedly feminine behaviours were still boys. Our age has somehow obscured this insight in favour of a retrenchment of stereotypes. One may wonder what is progressive about telling boys that masculinity means only these negative things, and nothing else. Surely it would be better for all to welcome more positive ideas of masculinity?

There may, at the cultural level, even be some strange kind of kudos and attraction in being a woman today. Novelist Fay Weldon, at nearly ninety, comments, somewhat naughtily, that 'It's more fashionable to be a woman. It seem[s] to me that women appear to be more powerful, at least among young men.'[21]

For Sigmund Freud, human sexuality and human sexual identity are not, as is often misunderstood, the same thing, though they are deeply intertwined. Freud suggests that all human sexuality is, despite reproduction, deeply tied up with the non-functional. Any form of sexual behaviour that is non-reproductive, which is to say, the vast majority of sexual behaviour, with or without another person – even, for example, a kiss – is, by definition, perverse. Even acts that result in conception may also be included in this category. Freud's radical understanding of human sexuality leads him to posit a fundamental bisexuality. This is to say not that we necessarily desire both women and men, although we might, but that all of our sexual being is composed of masculine and feminine traits, whatever these might be in any particular period.[22] Twenty years later, Freud will continue to make this claim: 'all human individuals, as a result of their bisexual disposition and of cross-inheritance, combine in themselves both masculine and feminine characteristics, so that pure masculinity and femininity remain theoretical constructions of uncertain content.'[23]

Freud's presentation of our founding bisexuality alerts us to the fact that sexual being and sexual desire are necessarily a psychological question before they are ever a physiological or anatomical one. This is to say that today to assume that one's identity as a sexed and sexual being is first and foremost a question only of our desire to be a sexual object for someone else (insofar as that desire exists) is to discount or negate the psychic dimension of desire. In our age, we sometimes mistake the object of desire for the desire itself. It is no wonder, then, that some seek to coincide with this object. Everything today seems to be a *thing*, which is to say an entity that can be possessed, exchanged, damaged, broken, returned, cared for, or abused. But to see one's own body as an object is to miss something fundamentally distinct from its objectness, which is to say its desire as such: and we do not coincide exactly with our desire.

If we are all *constitutively* bisexual, the door is open for a much more expressive and playful relation to various binaries and polarities: activity/passivity, dominance/submission, multiple kinds of acting, performing and pleasure.

Contemporary heterosexuality often seeks to suggest that one can find one's self, that is to say, one's self as an object, in the other, and that this romantic conception of fusion is somehow the solution to all personal and social ills. However, this wish puts far too much pressure not only on individual men and women but on romance and heterosexual being in general. What is missing, as I have tried to suggest so far, is a focus and a turn towards other modes of being together, a kind of *heterosociality* that is not overdetermined by the romantic or by the fear that all encounters between men and women must or should, at some level, be sexual. What is often absent in today's culture is a generalized friendliness, or concern for the other, *regardless of sex*.

Positive Masculinity?

Since its inception, feminism has, intentionally or otherwise, presented a challenge to masculinity. Increased female economic independence has transformed the relationship between men and women, with the latter no longer needing to rely on the former, just as capitalism transformed family structures from larger social networks to smaller nuclear family units.

As the twentieth century progressed, some men and men's groups strove to explore masculinity in ways that matched feminism's insights, but without straightforwardly simply opposing, or indeed completely accepting, the unfolding of women's liberation. Poet Robert Bly's *Iron John* (1990) is in many ways the template for attempts to critically salvage masculinity. Bly represents part of an attempt in the 1980s and 1990s to think about masculinity which prefigures some of today's positive discussions. He is associated with the 'mythopoetic' men's movement, which sought to use myth, therapy, Jung and other theorists of the unconscious to access deeper truths about manhood. He is in many ways a precursor to the figure of Jordan Peterson in his approach to the topic. As James Bloodworth characterizes Bly's legacy:

> Male discomfiture is increasingly audible today on YouTube, where Bly's ideological descendants mix Spartan asceticism with entrepreneurial uplift. It is traditionalism with a softer edge, in which self-development, stoicism, pseudo-scientific 'life hacks', and tips for developing rippling musculature sit alongside a new-age willingness to talk about feelings and vulnerability.[24]

The 1990s was interesting for its desire to deal in a thoughtful way with changes in the relationship between men and women. The mythopoetic movement sought to understand the changing roles of men and women, without sacrificing the possibility for a positive masculinity to thrive. Not everyone at the time agreed. As Jill Johnston wrote in *The New York Times* in 1992:

> Bly never grasped, it seems, the core concept of feminism, that the attributes of masculinity and femininity are cultural fabrications, rooted in a caste system in which one sex serves the other. You can tell he missed the point and instead imagined that feminism meant the idealization of 'the feminine', the reclamation of the Great Mother, when he says, 'More and more women in recent decades have begun identifying with the female pole, and maintain that everything bad is male, and everything good is female.'[25]

Not all feminists do agree that all attributes of masculinity and femininity are cultural fabrications, of course, and many feminists even at the time sought to reclaim the reality of female biology, and some did and still do want to celebrate the feminine – and why not?

In a 1982 interview entitled 'What Men Really Want', Bly notes a shift in the definition of masculinity from the 1950s onwards towards a certain kind of femininity in men:

> the women's movement encouraged men to actually look at women, forcing them to become conscious of certain things that the 80's male tended to avoid. As men began to look at women and their concerns, some men began to see their feminine side and pay attention to it. That process continues to this day, and I would say that most young males are involved in it to some extent.[26]

For men to pay attention to their feminine side would involve understanding what is necessarily being suppressed in the name of a narrow masculinity. It would involve reflecting on the role of the women in their life – their mother, sisters (biological or otherwise), lovers, friends, and so on. Bly's thought draws on the idea of masculine and female sides or aspects to the psyche. It's close to what Freud argued regarding constitutive bisexuality, and seems to me to be a far more thoughtful way of understanding our own character formation and how we might live in a more harmonious way, with ourselves as well as other people.

Today, though, we might find this sort of idea quaint or even slightly offensive – what does it mean to say we have masculine and feminine sides? Aren't we all *individuals* first and foremost? Perhaps. But, without denying the reality of male and female existence, we can perhaps wonder what it might mean to occupy an integrated position regarding 'feminine' and 'masculine' attributes. We are all somewhere in between. We all have aspects of our character and interests that place us somewhere between 'pure masculine' and 'pure feminine', regardless of sex.

As John A. Sanford puts it: 'Men are used to thinking of themselves only as men, and women think of themselves as women, but the psychological facts indicate that every human being is androgynous.'[27] Sanford was an Episcopalian priest as well as a Jungian, yet this claim sounds positively radical today, in an era in which gender roles and stereotypes seem completely locked down. To accept psychological androgyny is to admit that we are all more interesting than we might imagine.

We do not need to go so far as to believe, as people did in the sixteenth century, that we carry around a hidden part of the opposite sex in our body ('Our Adamic hermaphrodite, though he appears in masculine form, nevertheless carries about with him Eve, or his feminine part, hidden in his body'[28]) to wonder whether we are being cut off from a more integrated relationship with the various possibilities of our being. We encounter a paradoxical thought – a kind of basic androgyny shared by men and women that nevertheless includes and is predicated upon sexual difference. How this complex idea is handled tells us a great many things about every society that tries to wrestle with it, which is all of them.

While Bly is to some extent positive about the development of young men's 'feminine' side, he does however note that there is a sense of loss and sadness in the young men he talks to:

> I see the phenomenon of what I would call the 'soft male' all over the country today. Sometimes when I look out at my audiences, perhaps half the young males are what I'd call soft. They're lovely, valuable people – I like them – and they're not interested in harming the earth, or starting wars, or working for corporations. There's something favourable toward life in their whole general mood and style of living. But something's wrong. Many of these men are unhappy. There's not much energy in them.[29]

What energy is missing here, and why are these young men sad, according to Bly? In *Iron John*, his most famous text, Bly tells the story of the eponymous hero, an 1820 Grimm Brothers fairy tale which he suggests offers a 'third possibility' for men. In the story as Bly tells it, a young man and his dog venture out from a castle to a remote area of a forest, although the King had warned that people often don't return. They come across a pond, where the dog is pulled down under the water by a hand. Going back to the castle to fetch some buckets, the boy and other men empty the pond, finding at the bottom a 'large man covered in hair from head to foot'. The wild man's hair looks like rusty iron, hence the name 'Iron John'. They take him back to the castle and imprison him. The boy's ball one day rolls into Iron John's cage, the key to which lies under the Queen's pillow. Summoning up courage, the boy steals the key and unlocks Iron John, travelling into the forest with him for further adventures.

Bly writes: 'When a contemporary man looks down into his psyche, he may, if conditions are right, find under the water of his soul, lying in an area no one has visited for a long time, an ancient hairy man.'[30] To break with the maternal and embrace risk is not to straightforwardly 'renounce' the feminine, but rather to explore an aspect of masculinity that is submerged in a culture that encourages comfort and safety (there are, it must be said, plenty of women who are interested in taking risks too). The iron man, Bly suggests, is obscured by contemporary culture – he is hidden – though some men, and Bly mentions Freud, Jung and Wilhelm Reich – have done their best to uncover him. To be more like the Iron Man, Bly argues, is not to be 'macho' or cruel but, rather, to take forceful action with resolve. But first of all, you have to find this wildness within. In a world in which everything is increasingly online, nature does often seem far away: campaigns to 'rewild' humanity, by introducing children who live in the city to the countryside, have taken off in recent years. If we are to find ourselves again, as men or women or children, nature has to be a central part of this journey.

Bly suggests that this kind of feral, primal mentorship or initiation is profoundly lacking in Western culture – older men do not, as a rule, welcome 'the younger man into the ancient, mythologized, instinctive male world'.[31] Where might younger men get their wisdom from today? Men can only, ultimately, imitate men, Bly argues: 'Initiators say that boys need a second birth, this time a birth from men.'[32] Initiation into manhood has been eroded by a secular culture that sees no need to mark the passages of time, except in the most cursory way.

Bly is clear about the damage done by certain major historical changes: 'the love unit most damaged by the Industrial Revolution has been the father–son bond'.[33] Physical labour and father–son apprenticeships have, Bly suggests, disappeared or shifted under the weight of mother-domination and white-collar work. It is not a surprise that many men's rights activists often approvingly quote *Fight Club*'s Tyler Durden: 'We're a generation of men raised by women. I'm wondering if another woman is really the answer we need.'

Historic men's groups, such as the Achilles Heel collective, which produced a magazine of the same name to coincide with the London Men's Conference in 1978, criticized the essentialist idea that men could not change, and respected the observations feminism had made regarding labour, politics, families, and so on. As Vic Seidler, part of the collective that founded the group put it: '[Achilles Heel] recognized that many men had responded to feminism in a way that left them feeling guilty about themselves, as if the only option was to renounce masculinity itself.'[34] This explicitly socialist group, which engaged in its own consciousness-raising activity alongside feminist groups, took up the challenge of addressing the emotional issues specific to men, without resorting to the simplistic 'blame' narratives of today's male-shaming culture. Achilles Heel is a useful reminder that not all men's groups should be treated with suspicion or contempt: would that there were more opportunities for men to be honest and supportive of one another, the better to return to the heterosocial world.

Everyone needs someone to look up to. In the sorry absence of father figures, it is clear that in the post-industrial era a lot of men have turned inwards, towards self-reliance and physical strength. Interestingly, although some men get fit initially in order to be more attractive, fitness frequently becomes an end in itself. It often seems, looking at these men's journeys, that the more men engage in self-improvement, the less women are their central focus, and the more masculinity and friendships with other men become the most important thing.

What resources exist today for men to draw upon? The

mythopoetic movement that Bly was involved in continues in a revivified therapeutic culture, and in the attention paid to Stoic ideas by many men today. A few more recent books attempt a deeper kind of philosophical exploration of what it means to be a man. One such text is Ole Bjerg's 2020 book, *The Meaning of Being a Man*, in which Bjerg attempts to use the philosophers Martin Heidegger and Hannah Arendt, among others, to get at the heart of the question of 'Being-Man'; that is to say, to examine in depth the ontological and ethical meaning of manhood, including in relation to being with women.[35] As Bjerg puts it, emulating the often heavy style of German philosophy: 'Becoming Man is intimately interwoven with questions of what I can do together with Woman, what I should do with Woman, how I can be with Woman, how I want to be with Woman, and who I am with Woman.'[36]

Many other books about masculinity today are less ruminative, and more polemical, exhorting men to fight against contemporary 'feminizing' culture. *Masculinity Amidst Madness* falls into this category. Written by the possibly pseudonymous Ryan Landry ('a Middle American family man'), in short, stark sentences the author declares that today, 'Masculine values are attacked. The natural order of life is upended, and this upending is not for the benefit of women, but rather the elites who want dependent, weak people.' Landry attacks a world that appears to encourage boys to grow up without fathers. He exhorts men to study and learn, to turn away from contemporary media, to get fit, to 'develop strength', to work on friendships, to cultivate loyalty, to listen to religious leaders, to pray, to seek out beautiful art, to learn a trade, to become a leader, to deny male 'essence' to 'unworthy women', to remember ancestors, to hunt, to speak well, to join a *Männerbund* ('a group of men that is organized and aligned with male instincts and drives,' as Landry defines it, but which can more neutrally be translated as 'a male organization'), to support one another, and to accept nature and death.

Today, Landry suggests, 'Every single male virtue is treated as a vice for which we must repent and apologize.'[37]

Landry's defence of masculinity is traditionalist, conservative and heroic, predicated upon an idea of a lost manhood that must and can only be brought back by discipline in opposition to a permissive civilization, but there is no doubt an appeal in his words to a generation of men who feel out of sync with a world that seems to have 'moved beyond' these older values. It may seem easy to criticize what Landry and other pro-masculinist writers propose as the solution to today's 'sick society', but certainly there is much that can be criticized about a world that seems to want to punish men for striving to improve themselves.

Landry's and other masculinist texts do not, it seems to me, necessarily encourage misogyny. On the contrary, they describe a world in which men and women live and work together. A certain kind of metropolitan 'egalitarianism' would find this kind of traditionalism unpalatable, no doubt, but if 'equality' just means being equally crushable by the labour market and by an unhealthy culture, there's nothing to be gained there either, and nothing to be lost by turning one's back on modernity as such. There is also nothing progressive about encouraging a cynical, oppositional attitude between the sexes, or about blaming either sex for the misfortune and suffering of the other. If pro-masculinist books have an appeal to young men in particular today, it is in large part because they present an image of an escape from various kinds of depressed, morose types of masculinity in a consumerist, hedonistic society.

Masculinity and Physicality

There are many, often self-published, books, websites, Twitter feeds and videos specifically dedicated to improving the physical and mental health of men. Hunter Drew, for example, in *31 Days to Masculinity: A Guide to Help Men Live Authentic Lives*, writes:

> I'm writing solely for men who are looking to reclaim or pos-
> sibly for the first time discover their authentic *self*. Men who are
> not asking for permission to be who they are but rather choose
> to embrace their masculine nature and truly live this life, hope-
> fully that's *you* . . . You're a **Man**, more than that you're *the Man*
> and you're worthy of a life that consists of more than simply
> existing.[38]

Drew's *31 Days* is hardcore. Anyone undertaking it for the
thirty-one days (no get-outs) must not masturbate, 'edge', or
touch their penis for pleasure during the month (you can have
sex with someone else, though); must avoid porn; must do 100
push-ups every day; must start reading a new book, at least a
few pages a day; must give honest answers to questions ('start
telling the world your true opinion'); must give up any vices
such as alcohol or pot. Every day brings a new challenge (beyond
the 100 push-ups) along the lines of facing inner demons, break-
ing routines, giving up material possessions, and so on. In a
sense, the challenge transcends both sex and fitness: 'This isn't
about getting fit and it isn't about getting your dick wet, it's
about cultivating masculinity.'

This last point raises an interesting set of questions: what *is*
masculinity today, if it is not about sex and fitness? There is
something undoubtedly spiritual about Drew's *31 Days*, reflected
in the discipline, both mental and physical, it requires. Drew,
who served in the navy for eight years, alongside the disciplin-
ary aspects, emphasizes the sense of brotherhood it invokes:
'your masculine brothers are counting on you to join their sparse
ranks of authentic men in our society'.

Similarly, P. D. Mangan, a health and fitness guru ('I teach how to eat right, get strong, live long, and win, with science-based health and fitness'), tweets that: 'Two men, passing each other on the street, strangers to each other, give each other the nod. They're both in shape, and it's so rare now it feels like membership in a secret society.'[39]

There is a general feeling in the manosphere that fitness is not merely an end in itself, nor a means to attract women (the majority of health and fitness gurus are heterosexual men, though there is some crossover with gay male body-worship), but rather a quest for the holy grail of masculinity as such, which is at the same time a kind of solidarity with other men. It is about male confidence. According to Drew: 'This isn't about creating any type of caricatures, it's about men finding comfort in being men again. It's about tapping back into that genuine *I do not give a fuck* confidence that radiates from guys who own their shit and pursue their mission . . . I'm going to force you into the wild where masculine men run.'

Is there anything wrong with this image of masculinity? It is certainly good to feel physically fit, if one is able. In fact, we might ask, what is wrong with taking responsibility for your body and life, and changing things for the better? To be independent, to be fit and to think for yourself makes you better able to help others around you. It makes you less dependent on medication and addictive substances. It makes you less dependent on healthcare systems. Being fit improves your mood and your quality of life.

Let's put an end to whining, many of these men say, and let's eat vast quantities of meat while we're at it (many of the diets promoted in the manosphere involve few to no carbs, strategic fasting and whole foods). P. D. Mangan posts motivational tweets about diet that also function as pithy critiques of consumer capitalism and mental health:

You: 'Doc, I'm depressed.'

Also you: eats junk food, drinks soda, plays video games, 30 pounds overweight, sleeps 6 hours a night, works under fluorescent lights in a cubicle.

Doc: 'Here, have some of these pills.'[40]

The male tough talk that invokes a sense of personal responsibility for one's health, and, by extension, one's way of being in the world with others, shows up the passive acceptance that's widespread today, the slump into a certain kind of collective defeated misery.

Though capitalism might be to 'blame' for our sicknesses, capitalist 'solutions' (in the form of overmedication, and the overconsumption of harmful foods and substances) are also potentially unhealthy. But none of us has to accept these terms: if we learn what suits our body, understand what our limits are, work out when we can and look after ourselves, we find ourselves transformed into better people. It is not always easy to exercise, but it is always possible to ask oneself what the best way to live is, and endeavour to do it.

Beyond medication, there are contemporary 'cures' of a kind in the form of the various 'self-care' industries, where diet, cleansing and sleep all somehow become 'lifestyle choices', as opposed to basic techniques of sustenance and hygiene. Here we see the feminized counterpart to the manosphere's emphasis on meat and muscle – the bubble-bathification of women, the retreat into comfort and candles accompanied by the fantasy that this is some kind of radical gesture.

As Anne Dufourmantelle, who died in 2017 in an attempt to save two children from drowning, puts it in *Power of Gentleness: Meditations on the Risk of Living*: 'Theories of self-improvement and pursuit of happiness participate in spite of themselves in this grand marketplace of "well-being" that refuses to enter into negativity and confusion and fear as essential human elements, paralyzing the future as well as the present.'[41] The well-behaved contemporary individual is subject to his or her apps and avoids risk and excess at all costs. Separating out genuinely living well from fads, consumerist junk and ideological tricks is not easy, but it is possible to wend one's way skilfully through the bombardment of things that make you sick and things that make you well, even when the two seem proximate. It is objectively better for everyone that people are well, are encouraged to be healthy and not addicted. If we want to call this 'masculinity' when men do it, then so much the better. Women are as keen as men – if not more so – to know what wonderful things might follow from these positive changes.

4. The Games Men Play

Whether we like it or not, life is comprised of games: we play games with ourselves ('if the next car that comes around the corner is red, today will be a good day') and with each other – teasing, flirting, challenging. We don't always have a choice about some of what we do or have to do: not all of life can be playful. It is hard, for example, to see how needing to make enough money to survive can be easily 'gamified', though perverse employers might make a 'game' out of limiting how many times factory workers can visit the bathroom, or smoke a cigarette. Sometimes there seems little room for play, and everything seems like a chore. Even games can become a kind of work. But life can also involve enigmatic interactions, jokes, knowing references, curiosity, repeated hilarities and ambiguity. Often these are the most enjoyable aspects.

The etymology of 'game' is rather sweet, from the Proto-Germanic *gamann* meaning 'collective person', giving a sense of 'people together'.[1] Whatever games are, we may often feel that we are playing games not with others but more as loners forced to compete against everyone else, or tempted to give up on social life completely instead. We have been encouraged to become suspicious and untrusting.

What do games tell us about men? Ritualized games are often tied to ideas of what being a 'man' might mean, whether we're talking about football or boxing or any other kind of physical sport. And today everything is or can be 'gamified', which is to say, turned into something with rules, measurements and goals. You can make a game of your health, for example, by using an application on your phone or watch to count steps and give you 'rewards' (insurance companies can also gamify your health by giving you discounts for not smoking, going to the gym and not having pre-existing health conditions – but of course they can also punish you for being unhealthy). Life is increasingly lived as a claustrophobic game: games can be seen as supremely pointless or intensely exciting, real or unreal, welcome or enforced. In a rule-dominated world, leaving open space for uncertainty is inherently exciting: a closed world is a world without play and imagination.

In his great 1938 book, *Homo Ludens*, Johan Huizinga described man not as *Homo sapiens* (wise) nor as *Homo faber* (a maker), but as *Homo ludens*, 'Man the Player'. Huizinga suggests that 'all play means something' and that 'all play is a voluntary activity' (forced play is no play at all).[2] Play is also 'superfluous': it is not necessary for physical or moral reasons – it is pure enjoyment. It also has an important relation to meaning and earnestness: 'In play we may move below the level of the serious, as the child does; but we can also move above it – in the realm of the beautiful and the sacred.'[3] Some games between the sexes can – we must hope! – reach this level of the sacred. Huizinga is careful to separate out making love and playing, but acknowledges that even though the biological act itself 'does not answer to the formal characteristics of play', the 'road' to love is often 'made more enticing by all sorts of playing'.[4]

I want to suggest that it is possible to resurrect, engage and seriously enjoy (in however paradoxical a way) this 'road', amid the boringness of everything. This road may not even lead anywhere, nor does it have to. Love cannot be reduced to an algorithm! What should be fun has frequently become yet more work. Play and roughness are the very stuff of life: games between men and women have, from a certain perspective, often resembled war. Sometimes for the Greeks, for example, love was even the cause of war. But rather than regarding each other as alien creatures moving strange pieces on different boards, it would be far more enjoyable to enter into the spirit of adventure and experiment together. It may be that we *think* we know what we want – sex, fun, seriousness, children, a partner, a wife, a husband, a mother, a father – but we also *never really know* if what we want is indeed what we *say* we want. Life is very uncertain. The rules change all the time. We are all, at times, idiots. Sometimes we have to go back to the drawing board and come up with a new game. Let each one be lighter and more nimble than the last!

How many people enter into relationships of all kinds because they think that's what they *ought* to do, or because they think that not to do so would be strange, or because they are worried about what their parents or their friends might think? Or even what some anonymous 'other' might think? We may feel like we are autonomous beings, driving a clear path through and in companionship with our own, private desire. But we are all also inextricably tied up with the desire of others, and it is difficult to go up against social pressure, however much or little we have internalized it. Despite massive social shifts and the general acceptance of different family and romantic arrangements, we seem unable to fully let go of our worry in the face of this amorphous judgemental 'other'. Yet, on another level, we must know that this anonymous other (as opposed to the real people that surround us – those we know and care about one way or another) doesn't actually exist.

There is no collective group somewhere out there deciding how your decisions should be judged. God might be judging you, for sure, but regardless of any belief you might hold, becoming a consistently more elegant 'player of life' is something to aim for. I want to take seriously what Huizinga suggests regarding the seriousness of play and its relation to the beautiful and the sacred. What if all our relationships touched upon these realms? What if we overcame our anxieties and insecurities and embraced experiences of all kinds? What if we were the kinds of adults who could live freely and cope when confronted with difficulties – embrace the dynamism and trials of life?

Rather than playful beings, we are often encouraged today to be calculating beings, that is to say *to get the most we can as individuals*. This is a familiar idea in the current era of individualism which promotes self-interested behaviour across the board, from the economic to the personal. Trust has been eroded from all sides, we stand alone against everyone and we are supposed to *enjoy it*. Get what you can from the world before you die!

In the secular world, the toppling of God in the name of man, for all its progressive, modernist aspects, has rendered men and women unable, much of the time, to think about anything beyond themselves, about anything transcendent. Humanity has become the pinnacle and the measure of experience and desire, and so it follows that everything that we feel and want must be good simply because we feel and want (or believe that we want) it. This elimination of any reverence before the sacred is partly responsible for our romantic predicament: another person is supposed to be 'everything' to us, and yet they are in the same debased position we are. How can they be different enough for us to truly admire them? What love can be found among the ruins?

Another way of putting this is to revisit the idea of 'seriousness' in connection with play: a 'serious' relationship is one with several possible dimensions – it might be sexually exclusive, it might last a long time, it might involve children, it might be 'public' knowledge – that is to say, everyone 'knows' about its reality, which in turn reinforces this reality and confirms it. We are often upset when friends break up after a long-term relationship, even though we do not know how it might have been from the inside, or know what they might want that is different.

This is perhaps because the existence of their relationship oper-ated as a kind of reality principle for us too: if they exist together, it means that we *also* exist together, and that being in a couple is the *right thing to do* in general.

We might be taught to think of ourselves as individuals first and foremost, but we do not have to accept this very limited logic: games are collective enterprises whose outcomes are not assured. So we may as well enjoy them in the meantime! Is it possible to make the everyday, the mundane, the chore-like a thing of great joy and love? Perhaps! Or at the very least, it might be possible to arrange things so that there is more of one and less of the other, or to reorganize things so that resentment no longer features so heavily. In Ancient Rome, schools for children until the age of eleven were delightfully called '*ludus*'. Must everything today, even love, be approached in the spirit of regularity and weariness? Can we reorganize our lives, and the lives of children, so that we restore the relationship between ser-iousness and play?

Don't Hate the Player, Hate the Game: The Shifting Fortunes of Pick-Up Artists

Most of the games men play with women (and vice versa) are of limited kinds, usually involving blunt sexual approaches at a bar or via technology – a one-night stand, most predictably. It is not always clear whether women know the kinds of tactics some men employ when they are looking for a mate (whether for momentary fun or for a longer-term relationship): perhaps they should. It has to be said, in fairness, that men don't know what's going on with women either.

Sometimes, someone is using tactics on you when you are unaware that a game is even on. 'Pick-up artists' (PUAs) have always existed in one form or another, but they are the perfect example of a contemporary narrow type of game-playing between the sexes. Pick-up artists aim to seduce women using a variety of techniques – mixing up compliments and criticism, behaving boldly and therefore in an 'alpha' way, wearing down women's defences and going in for the kill. As 'Roissy', one of the leading contemporary PUAs, puts it in one of his maxims: 'When in doubt, ask yourself "WWJD?" What Would a Jerk Do? Then do that.'[5]

Social 'games', such as one-upmanship, subtle performances of power and coercion, and other forms of status manipulation and assertion, start to become more complicated: we often don't know we've been enlisted, and only later realize that perhaps we were 'played'. We might also be the ones playing games, even behind our own backs. Wherever there is sociability there are games: but there are also people deciding which type of game they are playing, and, indeed, what type of game they prefer. What happens when people playing a zero-sum game – where someone must lose – play games with unwitting partners who do not regard themselves as combatants? Yet this is often the situation when it comes to the pick-up game.

In a bestselling 2005 book, *The Game: Penetrating the Secret Society of Pickup Artists*, by Neil Strauss, 'the game' is approached somewhat obliquely. Rather than being a straightforward set of rules, it presents itself as an autobiographical account of the world of 'players'. It begins with the mental breakdown of star pick-up artist 'Mystery' as he experiences feelings of rage and suicidal despair, saying to a nurse at the hospital where the narrator, 'Style' (Strauss's pick-up name), has taken him: 'I know exactly what to say and what to do to make you attracted to me . . . It's all in my head. Every rule. Every step. Every word. I just can't . . . do it right now.'[6]

Strauss/Style is, by his own reckoning, an unattractive

man – balding, short, too skinny – yet by deciding to change his personality and develop an alter ego, he becomes popular with women. Beginning by looking into the burgeoning online pick-up community after someone suggests he turn a list of rules about picking up girls into a book, Strauss finds himself reminded of a frustration he suffers, namely that he 'can't seem to evolve to the next state of being because [he] spend[s] far too much time thinking about women'.[7] Strauss, through his investigations, goes from being a girl-less 'AFC' (Average Frustrated Chump) to being a successful man who can pick up women ('the alpha male I was never raised to be').

Encouraged to imagine interactions with women as video games, as 'not real', Style and the other aspiring picker-uppers are instructed in the art of the 'neg':

> Neither compliment nor insult, a neg is something in between – an accidental insult or backhanded compliment. The purpose of a neg is to lower a woman's self-esteem while actively displaying a lack of interest in her – by telling her she has lipstick on her teeth, for example, or offering her a piece of gum after she speaks.

This of course sounds improbable as a seduction technique, and it's ultimately not clear who looks worse when it succeeds: the men who use it or the women it works on. Freedom can be exhilarating, but it is also potentially cruel and stupid. It is not beyond our collective wit to think of better games than these, surely. Strauss, being a thoughtful kind of man, realizes that there are problems with this general mode of playing:

> It was then that I realized the downside to this whole venture. A gulf was opening between men and women in my mind. I was beginning to see women solely as measuring instruments to give me feedback on how I was progressing as a pickup artist. They

were my crash-test dummies, identifiable only by hair colors
and numbers – a blonde 7, a brunette 10. Even when I was having a deep conversation, learning about a woman's dreams and
point of view, in my mind I was just ticking off a box in my
routine marked 'rapport'. In bonding with men, I was developing an unhealthy attitude toward the opposite sex. And the most
troubling thing about this new mindset was that it seemed to be
making me more successful with women.[8]

A fair few years ago I happened to be in a bar where Neil Strauss
was talking about this book. It was, unsurprisingly, a largely
male audience. Strauss himself was a dynamic character in leather
trousers (or at least so memory convinces me) – charming and
witty in equal measure. It was easy to imagine him flirting at a
bar or club, or wherever these random encounters take place,
with some success. But it wasn't his description of the tactics of
'the game' that made him attractive, but rather his singularity, his
sense of humour, his way of being in the world. It may well be
possible to learn the rules of charisma: this is what those men
who make money trying to teach tactics to sexually unsuccessful
men promise. Women's magazines, too, similarly offer to instruct
women on how to pick up and 'keep' a man. But learning how to
manipulate someone into having sex with you, or even into falling in love with you, seems a bit cold. Seen from another angle,
though, we are constantly 'manipulating' each other – is it really
more ethical to learn from one's own mistakes rather than the
successes of others?

What does spontaneous flirting consist of, beyond the narrow-
ness of 'the game'? We might imagine it is more organic, more
attuned to the situation, more specific to the people involved.
Flirtation is complicated: we are not always sure where the
boundaries lie, and it usually involves risk and rejection. But it
seems a lot more subtle than the brute mechanical tactics whose

hollowness ultimately turns Strauss away (he later marries and writes another book, *The Truth*, about love and commitment).

For all of its limitations, its crassness, its mishmash of Neuro-Linguistic Programming, confidence tricks, twisted language and limited goals, we could nevertheless say that 'the game' in its original formulation at least required, of men, an open-ended relationship with other people. It involved speaking to strangers directly and running the risk of rejection or even violence from other men or from the women themselves. The situation today, a decade and a half after Strauss's book, seems very different, more homogenous. Dating apps have deferred the sting of real-world encounters, but they have also streamlined chance. In the heterosexual world of dating apps it is possible to vet in advance the type of person you might want to date – do you agree on the core issues of our time? Are you liberal or right-wing? Tall? Short? Do you smoke? Do you drink? Do you like cheese? Are you employed? Do you like Harry Potter? When 'matching' with someone in this way, before any actual physical encounter, in advance of any understanding of the way in which another person moves, speaks, smells or wanders through the world, we homogenize and pasteurize our relationship to the other. At the same time, we project an idealized image of ourselves – I am gregarious, funny, successful, all my friends say so! – and also of the other person: will you be a fun guy, a medium-to-long-term kinda guy, a bad boy, a husband, a father? Is this for sex or for life . . . or both?

By running our desire through computers we create closed worlds and loops that take us to a great extent out of risk and danger, but also move us away from possibility and randomness. The rationality of the filter precludes serendipity. It is possible to imagine a highly dystopian world – indeed, perhaps we already live in this world – where every encounter is mapped, recorded, documented and mediated by electronic means. This could protect us – our location is continually recorded – but it also creates a world which is heavily policed and where interactions that fall outside of these pre-ordained meet-ups are prohibited or discouraged. Why would you speak to a stranger in a bar when you could meet someone who already agrees with you on the death penalty in a chain coffee shop?

The desire and drive to document everything carries over into the personal – if we have sex with someone, does it make sense to record what happened the better to protect oneself against recriminations later down the line? In the wake of #MeToo, it might seem reasonable to avoid all forms of non-official, undocumented social and sexual contact, if only as an act of self-preservation. One company, LegalFling, 'the first blockchain based app to request and verify explicit consent before having sex', promises to create a 'legally binding agreement about sexual consent, which is verifiable through the blockchain'. The company writes:

> Sex should be fun and safe, but nowadays a lot of things can go wrong. Think of unwanted videos, withholding information about STDs and offensive porn reenactment. While you're protected by law, litigating any offenses through court is nearly impossible in reality. LegalFling creates a legally binding agreement, which means any offense is a breach of contract. By using the Live Contracts protocol, your private agreement is verifiable using the blockchain and enforceable with a single click.[9]

The app also promises to match your sexual preferences with those of your fling, which would entail, presumably, entering a list of your deepest fantasies into your phone – which seems, to put it mildly, a little weird, if not deeply foolhardy. It isn't clear, though, that the world is ready for such an app, most articles responding to the premise of LegalFling with scepticism and suspicion:

A blanketed contract ahead of engaging in sexual contact signals that consent is simply a one-time checklist. Consent, however, is something that occurs continually throughout a sexual encounter . . . People are allowed to change their minds – swiping 'okay' beforehand should not outweigh someone's discomfort during a sexual encounter, and it should certainly not be held to a higher legal standard.[10]

It is clear that such a development is double-edged, to say the least: we are in deep Charlie Brooker's *Black Mirror* territory here in any case. What happens to desire as such once it is completely captured by the machine? I don't believe that many people would really like a hackable record of their sexual history. At this point, we might not blame men and women from steering clear of contact, sexual or otherwise, altogether.

The Question of Touch

The repugnance to being touched remains with us when we go about among people; the way we move in a busy street, in restaurants, trains or buses, is governed by it. Even when we are standing next to them and are able to watch and examine them closely, we avoid actual contact if we can. If we do not avoid it, it is because we feel attracted to someone; and then it is we who make the approach. The promptness with which apology is offered for an unintentional contact, the tension with which it is awaited, our violent and sometimes even physical reaction when it is not forthcoming, the antipathy and hatred we feel for the offender, even when we cannot be certain who it is – the whole knot of shifting and intensely sensitive reactions to an alien touch – proves that we are dealing here with a human propensity as deep-seated as it is alert and insidious; something which never leaves a man

when he has once established the boundaries of his personality.
Even in sleep, when he is far more unguarded, he can all
too easily be disturbed by a touch.

Elias Canetti, *Crowds and Power*[11]

Even if humanity is not yet ready for a consent app, we have all
entered, whether we like it or not, into a relationship of desire
with the machine. We are touching objects more often than
we hold each other. What is being lost in this thing-world?

The typical smartphone user today touches his or her phone
2,617 times every day . . . extreme smartphone users – meaning
the top 10 per cent – touch their phones more than 5,400 times
daily.[12] Touch is positioned as the most difficult of possible human
interactions, because its meaning is intertwined with so many
layers of emotion. If we touch someone during a conversation, a
colleague who we know moderately well, say, on the arm, because
we want to reassure them, or support them, or because we want
also to reassure ourselves – along the lines that we are together in
this room at this moment and we have, or think we have, or at
least one of us does, a mild connection of friendship and affection, and a little touch is a microcosm of closeness – what does it
all mean? Might he or she find it inappropriate? How do we know
if someone wants to be touched? What if they misinterpret the
touch as something sexual when it was only meant kindly? What
if they react sexually in a way that surprises even themselves?
What if the toucher does too, involuntarily?

The discourse of 'consent' attempts to side-step this daily,
frequent, open-ended question, but, like all discourses, it brings
with it a whole host of other unforeseen and unintended consequences. Rather than translate my desire to touch my colleague's
arm into words ('Is it OK if I touch your arm?'), which would
sound utterly strange, and might be greeted with bafflement of

varying degrees ('But of course!' or 'Why are you asking?!' or 'Er, I guess?' or 'If you like!' or 'What an odd request!', or simply 'No!'), it would be easier to simply not attempt what would otherwise be a passing gesture.

So we increasingly end up in a world in which no one touches anyone else, apart from in the most closed settings, even when we would want to reassure, be kind, express solidarity, friendship or affection, but at other times to express aggression, attraction, flirtation, desire – because getting it wrong is a nightmare. Touch is a touchy subject, precisely because the stakes are simultaneously so low and so high. Touch always has the capacity to be violent rather than gentle. 'To stroke' and 'to strike' share the same etymology.

In a 2015 article entitled 'No Touching: The Countries That Dislike Physical Contact the Most' with the subheading 'A study suggests you should hug a Finn, but not a Brit', Aamna Mohdin reported that

> participants, from Finland, France, Italy, Russia, and the U.K., detailed where strangers, family members, friends, and romantic partners were allowed to touch them . . . For almost everyone, the hands are OK. Unsurprisingly, no one wanted relatives of either gender to touch their genitals. And, regardless of nationality, researchers found that the closeness of the relationship correlated with the range of areas that can be touched.[13]

The authors of the original study remarked, 'Nonhuman primates use social touch for maintenance and reinforcement of social structures, yet the role of social touch in human bonding in different reproductive, affiliative, and kinship-based relationships remains unresolved.'[14] We are conflicted, afraid, confused, stuck between animals and angels, laughing nervously, stepping aside, anxious not to offend, yet desperate not to be left alone.

Humanity possesses great imagination when it comes to sexual desire and envisaging possible relationships: we generate all manner of images to stimulate ourselves, recreating scenes we may have been lucky enough to live through at one time or another, or projecting images of situations we might never actually experience. Our mind is one great cinematic enterprise, and is constantly being refilled and replenished with new one-act plays or B movies.

The trouble is that we are, unless we are careful, flooded with images from outside, particularly ones that stimulate our desire. Images are always potentially dangerous: we often do not know where they come from, who wants us to see them, the effect they have on us and how we might seek to emulate them, consciously or unconsciously. Sometimes particular images get 'stuck' and we become completely beholden to them: these can be images of another person that we might want to be, or might desire (whether realistically or otherwise).

It is also extremely easy to get addicted to particular types of images: whatever moral position we might take in relation to the unutterably large amount of freely available pornography that the internet provides (and there are many theories as to why such a large amount exists, and in whose interest is it that it does: who benefits from such a situation?). Some young men increasingly suffer from the 'death grip' of excessive masturbation and many people's expectations of sex are shaped more or less completely by pornography. The reality, if there is even any longing left for sexual encounters with real bodies, is then something of a shock.

Most pornography is directed towards men: why is that? Men are supposed to have a more visual relation to desire. It is generally supposed that men respond more readily to visible stimuli whereas women are supposed to feel more moved by narrative. One study puts it like this:

Evidence supports that some previously observed sex differences in response to sexual stimuli may, in part, reflect a differential response to the content of the stimuli used. Men are influenced by the sex of the actor portrayed in the stimulus while contextual factors, possibly allowing for the creation of a social scenario, may be more important to women.[15]

But it strikes me that, visual questions aside, there are a lack of good stories today for either men and women – particularly concerning intimacy. Masturbation with pornography creates a particular kind of loop, one that by definition excludes the other: are we, then, in a relationship only with ourselves? Even if we 'match' with another via an app, we might simply end up mediating our masturbation through the body of the other. What is specific and unique about our encounters disappears if everything is formulated in advance.

In a piece entitled 'Why Are Young People Having So Little Sex?', a well-received article about the apparently burgeoning 'sex recession', author Kate Julian points out that between 1991 and 2017, the US Centers for Disease Control and Prevention's Youth Risk Behavior Survey found that the percentage of high-school students who'd had sex dropped from 54 to 40 per cent. In other words, she says, 'In the space of a generation, sex has gone from something most high-school students have experienced to something most haven't.'[16] Julian suggests that this may be a broader indication of a 'withdrawal from physical intimacy that extends well into adulthood'.

We are entering a phase in which the possibility of adulthood is increasingly out of reach. More people stay in education longer, get more in debt and have less opportunity to achieve the classical markers of adulthood – marriage, children, property ownership. Even though human biology is real, and fertility for women declines sharply after thirty, the culture keeps saying that being forty is the new twenty, twenty the new ten, ninety the new seventy, and so on . . .

Julian's research involved listening to multiple theories about the 'sex recession':

> I was told it might be a consequence of the hookup culture, of crushing economic pressures, of surging anxiety rates, of psychological frailty, of widespread antidepressant use, of streaming television, of environmental estrogens leaked by plastics, of dropping testosterone levels, of digital porn, of the vibrator's golden age, of dating apps, of option paralysis, of helicopter parents, of careerism, of smartphones, of the news cycle, of information overload generally, of sleep deprivation, of obesity. Name a modern blight, and someone, somewhere, is ready to blame it for messing with the modern libido.[17]

We might indeed wonder about all of these things, and about the relationship between modern life and the possibility of sex. We might go deeper into thinking about how our desire gets shaped precisely by modern life itself, by our phones and computers, and about what happened to all that time we used to have. We might ask a larger historical question about the meaning of all of this.

Have men and women simply had enough of sex? If we map the sexual revolution of the 1960s onto other historical revolutions, let's say the French Revolution, we would expect a period of rapid and excessive libidinal activity, a culture becoming saturated by sex, followed by a period – the Terror – in which the originators of the original revolution are beheaded (or castrated), then another more balanced period (Thermidor), in which things even out slightly. #MeToo can easily be seen as the 'Terror' phase, as an entire culture comes to terms with its collective 'walk of shame' and seeks scapegoats for its previous excesses. It may well be that we are entering into a new phase of neo-traditionalism in which the sexual revolution, and the backlash against it, are superseded, at least in part because of the anxieties generated by technology, and we move once again towards monogamous relationships in which libidinal energy is more or less contained. Where the allure of dating apps has worn off in favour of long-term commitment. But at the same time, where 'sex' has become increasingly virtualized, screen-based. A post-real-sex age, perhaps.

The End of Pornography?

In December 2020, Pornhub, the world's biggest porn site, removed the majority of its content – moving from hosting 13 million to 4 million videos – following a *New York Times* report revealing that the site was hosting footage of child sexual abuse and trafficking victims. Credit card companies Visa and Master-card cut ties with the site.[18] This moment marks something of an interesting turn in what seemed to be an unstoppable deluge of pornographic content.

Let's assume that we're heading towards a post-sexual revolu-tionary era. Nevertheless pornography dominates, despite these crack-downs. Many men struggle with the widespread availabil-ity of porn. Even apart from the destruction of the capacity for fantasy it induces, and the abuse of those men and women who act in it, there's no doubting porn's capacity to be addictive, not to mention the way it shapes sexual behaviour and expectation in real-life encounters.

All pornography reveals what philosopher John Locke real-ized but hoped he could hold off with the promise of God. He argued that our bodies are our 'own' (i.e. our property, with which we can do what we like), but we should avoid treating them badly because they are *also* the property of God. Capitalism is therefore Locke without God. The body is everything, but we exist only insofar as we exist as beings that can capitalize on our sexual existence. What resistance is possible when the 'revolution' itself claims freedom as its own? Nevertheless, despite its domination, pornographic capitalism does not have the monopoly on liberty. There are ways of being free that turn their back on 'liberation' as it was sold to humanity in the second half of the twentieth century. To control one's desire is no less a form of freedom, and is arguably far greater than being hooked on something harmful.

NoFap

In recent years, there has been a small but significant reaction against the excesses of pornography. This counter-movement comes not from anti-porn feminists or religious organizations, but from men. 'NoFap', which emerged in around 2011, is a movement that helps men (overwhelmingly) move away from porn and masturbation. These men want to do this for a variety of reasons – among which are concern with the addictive nature of the medium and a desire to cut down on self-pleasuring. Some worry that porn-use reduces their drive and their ability to have a relationship with women that isn't shaped by the pornographic gaze. 'Fapstronauts' aim to abstain from 'PMO' (pornography, masturbation and orgasm) for a period of time, often ninety days, in order to 'reset' their brain and to reclaim their freedom. In NoFap communities, you see men supporting one another in giving up: 'I hope one day I can get as high as 10,000 days porn free.'[19] Their Reddit forum's slogan is, fittingly, 'get a new grip on life'.[20] The NoFap movement is related to men's rights activism, but with a particular focus on self-improvement. In this respect it's pointed, we could say, at a certain form of 'toxic masculinity' but in a more internalized and self-critical way. It is a rejection of the domination of technology and the sexualization of everyday life. NoFappers speak about 'rebooting' their brains – that is to say, resetting or recalibrating their sexual desire back to its 'factory setting'.

It's interesting to note that the computer imagery here moves from the medium that supplies the problem, in other words, pornography on the internet, to the image of a pristine machine that can be restarted as if newly taken out of the box. 'If you think of the sexual system as pressurized,' writes one messageboard user, 'and there is a specific way in which it is supposed to be released – but someone keeps coming along and draining the energy before it hits the critical mass – the system will never function as it should.'[21]

According to men who have successfully gone through NoFap – a period of at least ninety days of abstinence from any form of sexual contact – multiple benefits follow, from a renewed appreciation of the small things in life, to increased energy and mental clarity. Women are appreciated for their beauty and character without immediately being seen through the lens of the pornographic eye. The practice of semen retention has a long history, in tantra, Chinese alchemy and other forms of spiritual bodily practice. But in the case of NoFap, the first step is simply turning one's back on the all-too-available weight of sexualized images.

Some NoFappers even avoid using the word 'porn', preferring instead to spell it out in individual letters, as if its talismanic power was too strong. We could ask if they're not right to do so. What does porn do to people, actors and viewers? It distances people from each other, creates impossible and upsetting images and fantasies, and in the case of some men, generates patterns of addiction that lead to depression, inertia and an inability to connect socially, let alone sexually with others, especially the opposite sex, who become mere functions in a pornographic vision. It seems difficult to imagine our world without pornography, yet many have managed to eliminate it from their visual and physical field.

Conversation, joking, flirtation, graceful play – many of the NoFappers discuss how life returns in these ways post-porn. A liberated world is liberation from the tether of unreal, monstrous, endless screens. To enjoy one's sexuality is to have control over it, to not be its victim. The NoFap movement inadvertently reveals too the degree to which men may have a more precise idea of what constitutes 'toxic' kinds of masculinity than women. In a world in which men are systematically encouraged by powerful internet algorithms and by pick-up culture to be jerks (and to jerk off relentlessly), it is perhaps no surprise that there would be a rebellion by and for men against the mass manipulation of internet pornography. Part of becoming a better man is not wasting one's energy fruitlessly. It is much better, always, to conserve energy in order to deploy it decisively in contexts where it is needed.

The most destructive games men play are ultimately with themselves – selfish, masturbatory games. Such games might involve women superficially, as in the games of the pick-up artists, but they are also, in fact, self-referential phenomena. Men sometimes close themselves off in onanistic loops. But these are sad, depressing games, not joyful, liberating modes of playing. There is far more delight in real games, serious games that nevertheless retain a lightness of spirit, than can be found alone in front of a screen.

5.   Is Separatism the Answer?

> There is one fear, above all others, that unites men in
> what we have come to regard as modern masculinity.
> It's a fear that affects almost all men, whether they are
> meek and timid by nature or the kind of men who walk
> into burning buildings to save people's lives . . . That
> fear is the fear of losing a woman's love and approval.
> It is a fear so deep and so pernicious that men will go
> to insane lengths to preserve the illusion of love, even
> when being bitch-slapped with the fact that the love
> isn't there and never was.
>
> Paul Elam, *Men. Women. Relationships.*[1]

Male and female interaction is an awkward and confusing
mess, where the rules are often extremely obscure. Sexual liberation, secularism, consumer capitalism and the constant
awakening and jangling of multiple desires on the basis of the
circulation of images and ideas, pornographic or otherwise,
have generated conflict between the sexes – or at least the
appearance of conflict because these 'battles' are sometimes
overplayed, and other times underplayed, so we do not see
them as they really are.

In our quest to determine, impossibly, *what men want*, it is
instructive to look towards the extremes: what do men say
about themselves and about women when they veer towards the
edges, towards the abyss? It is very easy to dismiss and denounce
some, or even all, men as 'misogynist' and 'sexist', and no doubt

there are a very few men who do pathologically hate women. But these men are rare, and we all instead exist somewhere in the middle, sometimes blaming individual men or women for our troubles, sometimes the entire sex, and sometimes the universe as a whole. Or, if we're lucky, we've transcended the blame game, perhaps by accepting that life is unfair, nothing is perfect, we all make mistakes, and that forgiveness is possible, indeed necessary!

How much should men and women hang out together? What, if any, time and space should they have to themselves, or with their own sex? It's not at all clear that there has ever been any resolution to the question of whether men and women can be friends, even when in practice it is clear that they often are – some of my best friends are men! We might laugh at US Vice President Mike Pence claiming, on the basis of the so-called 'Modesto Manifesto' inaugurated by preacher Billy Graham, that 'he never eats alone with a woman other than his wife and that he won't attend events featuring alcohol without her by his side',[2] and we might wonder if women in politics could ever make the same decision without their career stalling, but we might also feel uneasy: what *is* the right level of social or friendly interaction between men and women?

What is surprising is how little thought we give today to what positive relationships between men and women, particularly outside romantic or sexual attraction, could be like. It is surely possible to defend an eminently twenty-first century idea of male–female friendship *despite*, precisely, the cynicism and scepticism which usually greets the idea ('Men and women can't be friends! One of them will always want to fuck the other! Partners will get jealous', and so on). Life is strange and interesting. It is all the more interesting to discuss it with people who are a bit like, but not exactly like, yourself.

We can, in any case, always decide against spending time

together. Everyday heterosocial life involves multiple kinds of interactions with the opposite sex, even if we might be doing our best to avoid them. Some of these relationships are fleeting but polite, some kind, some funny, some confusing, some affectionate, some flirtatious, some uncomfortable, some hostile, and so on. Clearly it depends on who we are and how we are perceived as to how we might be treated, and there are always going to be serious mismatches in the level of interest – social, sexual – that one person might receive compared to another, which undoubtedly leads to resentment. We must remember that sexual desire is unfair. Some people are very beautiful, others are not. There is a naturally unequal distribution of attractive qualities of all kinds, though there is also quite a lot anyone can do to improve themselves, intellectually or physically – this indeed is the promise of much of the upbuilding narratives of masculinist literature. Nevertheless, this terrible truth of asymmetrical attractiveness clashes with other aspects of contemporary ideology: that everyone is equal, at least formally. The market – all markets – suggests that we should always be able to get what we want. But what if what we want is unattainable? What if it is bad for us? What if desire is sometimes highly destructive of the common good? A society run purely on *what people want* is going to encounter serious difficulties, since desires will always clash.

The Unjust Economics of Sex

The French novelist Michel Houellebecq repeatedly raises the problem of sexual injustice in his novels and interviews. His characters are often men bereft of female contact, or men who pay for sex with women. In his first novel, translated into English as *Whatever*, the narrator writes:

Some men make love every day; others five or six times in their
life, or never. Some make love with dozens of women; others
with none. It's what's known as 'the law of the market' . . . Economic liberalism is an extension of the domain of the struggle,
its extension to all ages and all classes of society. Sexual liberalism is likewise an extension of the domain of the struggle, its
extension to all ages and all classes of society.[3]

It is this double law – market values and sexual values that create
widespread division and inequality – which leads to much of
today's resentment between the sexes, particularly in heterosexual men who never or rarely have relationships or sexual
encounters with women.

Houellebecq's concern, as academic Douglas Morrey suggests, is not with the unfettered sexual liberation promised by
his parents' feckless post-war generation, but rather with 'a
world without sex'.[4] It is a world in which one's value and status
are measured primarily by one's sexual prowess. Some of these
men blame feminism for their lot in life, but they are not wrong
to understand that, from an economic point of view, they are
becoming increasingly obsolete. So much of contemporary culture is polarized and blinkered. But we will never improve life
for anyone, let alone everyone, if we do not understand why
people feel the way they do, whether we think they are correct
or not.

We live in a time, as Houellebecq suggests, after the sexual
liberation of the 1960s, in which we do not really know what to
do. The market has become the model for everything: romance
is treated as much like an economic exchange as possible. In the
world of the manosphere, men and women each have an 'SMV'
(Sexual Market Value) and women are seen as hypergamous –
always seeking to 'marry up', to a man who has a higher social
and sexual status than their own. This undoubtedly leads to

some fairly derogatory thinking regarding women. On 'The Red Pill' forum, for example, one commentator writes:

> The thing with women is their preferred SMV changes throughout their cycle depending on their hormone balance at the time (days 5–15 it's badasses, at other times it's richasses). Also, women tend to have a handsome-enough litmus before other criteria start taking over.[5]

This kind of diagnosis of what women want (and what men want) is common online – trying to make sense of the uneven distribution of sexual fulfilment. Some men, undoubtedly, feel entitled to more sexual recognition than they currently get. But can sex ever be a demand or an expectation along the line of other basic needs?

In the wake of Elliot Rodger's murderous attack in 2014 and the rise of incel culture, philosopher Amia Srinivasan wrote a piece entitled 'Does Anyone Have the Right to Sex?'[6] She defines the incel as 'a certain kind of sexless man: the kind who is convinced he is owed sex, and is enraged by the women who deprive him of it'. Rodger's final manifesto, 'My Twisted World', was explicit on this point: 'All I ever wanted was to fit in and live a happy life . . . but I was cast out and rejected, forced to endure an existence of loneliness and insignificance, all because the females of the human species were incapable of seeing the value in me.'[7] Noting that the 40,000-member Reddit incel forum was closed down in 2017 for violating the site's policy on calling for violence, Srinivasan argues that Rodger misunderstood the reality of patriarchy, which allows for multiple types of attractive man but very little variation in what counts as an attractive woman.

What Srinivasan taps into is the question that also motivates this book – the question of desire, and male desire in particular. Feminism, Srinivasan suggests, is no longer up to the job of thinking about this question ('It used to be the case that if you wanted a political critique of desire, feminism was where you would turn'). Tracking the relationship between sex-critical and sex-positive feminism, Srinivasan reaches much the same conclusion as Houellebecq and those men who talk about SMV, namely that the market has permeated sex completely:

> Sex is no longer morally problematic or unproblematic: it is instead merely wanted or unwanted. In this sense, the norms of sex are like the norms of capitalist free exchange. What matters is not what conditions give rise to the dynamics of supply and demand – why some people need to sell their labour while others buy it – but only that both buyer and seller have agreed to the transfer.[8]

There are plenty of people, beyond frustrated young men on the internet and French novelists, who understand that today sex is a marketplace like everything else, but also that life is unfair. Instead of mourning the absence of something, what about leaving sex behind? Why not dwell in the gentler pleasures of friendship, or take leave of the opposite sex altogether? From incel to volcel (voluntary celibate) . . .

Separation as Solution

There are men today who, absolutely tired of the pressures of the marketplace of compulsory heterosexuality, seek to opt out of relations with the opposite sex, insofar as this is possible. In recent years, loosely affiliated groups of men have sprung up who profess an earnest desire to have nothing to do with women. Among the largest is 'Men Going Their Own Way' (MGTOW), which has around 66,000 subscribers on Reddit. MGTOW envisages life without women, including marriage and children.

Its adherents generally do not date. MGTOW's logo is a road on a yellow background with a side road splitting off from the main road, indicating a 'swerve' away from the 'normal' path.

MGTOW.com carries this statement of intent:

> M.G.T.O.W – *Men Going Their Own Way* – is a statement of self-ownership, where the modern man preserves and protects his own sovereignty above all else. It is the manifestation of one word: 'No'. Ejecting silly preconceptions and cultural definitions of what a 'man' is. Looking to no one else for social cues. Refusing to bow, serve and kneel for the opportunity to be treated like a disposable utility. And, living according to his own best interests in a world which would rather he didn't.
>
> In other words . . . *common sense for men.*[9]

One of the interesting things about MGTOW's guiding statement is the way in which it echoes earlier decades of feminist work. Saying 'No' and refusing gender stereotypes ('silly preconceptions and cultural definitions of what a "man" is') were key feminist demands of the second wave. Similarly, refusing to submit to authority and maintaining personal and bodily integrity very much characterizes second-wave feminist demands: 'my body, my choice'.

How, then, to understand the positions and feelings of those men who resent women? How to understand those men who seek, either as a result of this resentment, or through indifference, to exit encounters with women altogether? The key here lies in attempting to imagine a different relationship between men and women that would not reduce them to their 'value' on the sexual marketplace. An honest world would acknowledge the awkward-at-times inseparability of men and women in various kinds of positive relationships that include friendship (not just seen as a 'consolation prize').

Is MGTOW a brave assertion of male sovereignty in the face

of women who are deemed to seek only money, security, children and status, or is it rather a way of rationalizing other desires – to spend more time with other men, or to protect oneself from heartbreak? Are women really exploiting and oppressing men on such a large scale? Male separatism, as extreme as it sounds, might today make a certain kind of perverse sense, given that the options for 'being together' in the contemporary world sometimes appear so unattractive. Besides the obvious point that without reproduction there would be no more humans to even be annoyed by each other, there seems a curious nobility in some men giving up on women, so long as it is done without bitterness.

MGTOW are not exactly traditionalists, although there is some overlap with men who express a strong and serious desire to return to older-style relations, however imaginary, between the sexes, for religious reasons or otherwise. It is also revealing to look at the parallels between male separatism today and the female version of the 1970s (which we should note was never the mainstream thrust of second-wave feminism). What does, and could, a man who seeks to exit female company have in common with a lesbian who shuns the male world in favour of her sisters – sexually, politically, emotionally, economically? Something they do share is historical roots in the withdrawal from the world of intra-sex relations practised by religious hermits, nuns, monks, anchorites and others over the centuries.

There were and are always men who would prefer to spend time alone or with other men, regardless of sexual orientation, and some women too who prefer the company of women. There have historically been plenty of solitary men, men who never married, men who were gay or who chose – sometimes for scholarly or religious reasons – to have nothing to do with women. At different times in history, men and women had far fewer 'shared spaces', coming together only for reasons of arranged marriage

or at festivals. Women would have worked together with other women, men with other men. This gendered division of labour no longer exists today in a world in which employers are largely indifferent to the sex of their workers.

But the essentially *reactive* nature of today's male separatism is clear: 'If MGTOW is fire, then perhaps feminism is gasoline.'[10] Citing Newton's Third Law of Motion ('For every action there is an equal and opposite reaction'), the supposed malevolence of contemporary feminism crops up everywhere in MGTOW-land. One poster on the site shows a woman chained to a bear-trap with a heart inside as a man looks on: 'It's a trap!' MGTOW argues that 'survival and mating' are mere animal behaviours and that men could do much better, that is to say, exit relations with women in the name of a higher calling:

> For millennia, men have accomplished and contributed far greater miracles of science, discovery and human endeavour, and thanks to men like Orville and Wilbur Wright, man is the only mammal that can't fly – that CAN fly. Man is also the only species that has the capability of deflecting an extinction-level event.[11]

This rather elevated sentiment is borne out to some degree by the high proportion of 'successful' men in history who have never married. As Nietzsche says in *The Genealogy of Morality*:

> Which great philosopher, so far, has been married? Heraclitus, Plato, Descartes, Spinoza, Leibniz, Kant, Schopenhauer – were not; indeed it is impossible to even think about them as married. A married philosopher belongs to comedy, that is my proposition: and that exception, Socrates, the mischievous Socrates, appears to have married *ironice*, simply in order to demonstrate this proposition.[12]

There is truth in the idea that some male scholars and thinkers turn away from marriage and children in the name of innovation, thought or creation of other kinds – recall Cyril Connolly's infamous statement: 'There is no more sombre enemy of good art than the pram in the hall.'

Are there contemporary women's movements comparable to MGTOW? There is a nascent WGTOW movement, but it is not clear that it corresponds to much widespread sentiment among women. There is a WGTOW Reddit community (with 6,200 members as of January 2021 and a motto: 'WGTOW is a community of women supporting other women who wish to live independently from men and relationships with them')[13] and some discussion on 'Red Pill Women' about the idea, with one commentator suggesting that

> WOMEN can absolutely go their own way. In fact, women going their own way is what started all the changes in our culture that led, many, many years later, to movements like the Red Pill and MGTOW that grew up from the muck that women left behind them . . . MGTOW is really just a reaction to many, many years of increasingly oppressive feminist doctrine. The feminist doctrine tells women to go their own way, i.e., in the famous mantra, 'You don't need no man!' And that is what women have been doing, in one way or another, since the 60s. TL,DR: WGTOW is feminism, and we live in a feminist society, so (nearly) all women are WGTOW.[14]

There is no need for a WGTOW movement, because women going their own way is already the dominant culture, at least since the widespread use of birth control, the commentator suggests. This claim is often echoed in the manosphere's emphasis on 'gynocentrism' – the idea that society privileges and prioritizes women over men. We are confronted, once again, with two implacably opposed ideas: that of 'patriarchy', and that of 'gynocentrism'. The gap between the extremes of what men and women are thinking about sexual relations could not be wider. It proves instructive at this point to examine the earlier women's separatist movement to understand where the impetus for separation came from, even though the motivation was quite different.

So, what, in recent history, was female separatism? For some women, it was simply a desire to discuss ideas away from men (think of consciousness-raising groups, where women could speak freely to other women about their struggles). Some women organized cultural events for women only. Some women strove to detach themselves from men completely, living with other women, and having nothing to do with the male world. Separatism wasn't solely practised or desired by lesbians; and of course not all lesbians are or were separatists. One of the earliest feminist separatist groups, 'Cell 16', did not see the solution in lesbianism, politically chosen or otherwise, advocating celibacy and martial arts instead.[15] Sexism within left-wing movements in the 1960s and 70s created the desire for women-only groups, though this in turn sometimes conflicted with the universalist aspects of left-wing principles ('Aren't we all working class?' 'Won't focusing on sex divide us further?').

Whatever MGTOW think, it is difficult to imagine a totally women-dominated world, which is not to say that women don't have power or are merely pawns or puppets in the game of patriarchy. It is true, nevertheless, that many men feel that it is *they* who are the victims of women's machinations, as MGTOW, at the extremes, indicates. What hope, then, for relations between men and women?

We already have friendships with each other, on the basis of shared interests and mutual admiration. These alliances may be strategic and political at times, but they are also not prey to the extreme ends of market valuation in the same way as romantic and sexual exchanges might be. There are degrees of separation: while men and women should be free to associate with whoever they choose, separatism tends to flatten out complexity, denouncing in turn all women as 'hypergamous' on the one hand and all men as 'bastards' on the other. If we do not wish to have romantic associations with one another, there are many other things we can discuss and enjoy together without unnecessary hostility. As Epicurus, who admitted men and women into his Garden school of philosophy, wrote: 'Friendship dances around the world, bidding us all to awaken to the recognition of happiness.'[16]

Men and women *need* each other, not only for reproductive purposes where these pertain, but in order to make sense of the universe, or to stand together in the face of absurdity. Can we in fact live without each other? I do not think so.

But there are moments when the promise of relating to one another no longer seems enough. There are forms of aloneness so profound that they cause deep depression, self-destruction and suicide. I want to finish this section on separatism by turning to the most serious dimension of men's current predicament – the fact that, as noted earlier, suicide is the leading cause of death of men under forty-five. Why is this? Why are some men driven to such extreme behaviour, and how can we all collectively help to reduce this terrible statistic?

Male Suicide

No single theory will untangle an act as ambiguous
and with such complex motives as suicide.

Al Alvarez, *The Savage God*[17]

In his 1971 book on suicide, *The Savage God*, Al Alvarez describes the death of his friend Sylvia Plath with stark and piercing clarity. Plath invites Alvarez over on Christmas Eve 1962. He stays for a drink and critically discusses a line in one of her poems 'The nude / Verdigris of the condor'. Alvarez tries, obliquely, to take the edge off of Plath's 'private horrors', but also avoids taking on responsibilities that he doesn't want and couldn't, 'in [his] own depression, have coped with'. When he leaves at around eight to go to a dinner party he understands that he has let her down 'in some final and unforgiveable way'. 'And,' Alvarez adds, 'I knew she knew.'[18]

Alvarez is describing the death of a woman whose life and work are now irreparably read through the lens of suicide. The suicide of someone you knew intensely and joyfully for a blessed and scarcely now imaginable period of time, participating in a cascade of thoughts and investigations, is, in every way, unbearable. Suicide never ends, it just gets folded like a pebble into the hem of days; it is a heavy fact, each recall, voluntary and involuntary, a drop into deep stitching, the fabric of hours. We might be able, in more elevated moments, to summon memories, to speak to the dead, to imagine what they might say, to find them in rare crossings in the ether; more often we feel their sadness, try to imagine their motives, feel our own sense of loss, our own remorse. It is true that no one really dies until the last person that remembers them is also dead, yet the death of someone you loved weighs like a flat stone, it is heavy, it is one-way.

As noted earlier, in the United Kingdom suicide is the biggest killer of men under forty-five, and 75 per cent of suicides are male.[19] In 2019, 4,903 men took their own lives.[20] It is impossible to talk about men and masculinity today without consideration of this fact. It is important at the same time to note that to discuss male suicide is not to diminish the anguish and pain of women who also suffer in this way.

Some have stressed the supposed inability of men to discuss their feelings, particularly those that touch upon questions of status, of inner misery, and of doubts and anxieties that may be felt to be laughable in the clear light of day. Yet male suicide perhaps may be felt differently in some ways. First among these is the question of what it means to feel so alone, *as a man*, against and not 'in' the world. How to understand this peculiarly isolated mode of being? This is what Mark Fisher, the writer and my friend who took his own life in 2017, described, half-jokingly, as 'the solitary urinal of male subjectivity'.[21]

The cult pseudonymous writer Zero HP Lovecraft (@0x49fa98) wrote something similar in a tweet on 30 October 2018: 'The component of male lived experience that is wholly unaccessible [*sic*] to women, more than any other, is the colossal and abyssal apathy of the universe towards you.'[22] Many men I have spoken to feel this way, at least sometimes. A feeling of total and abject aloneness before the void. Do men feel this cosmic apathy more than women do? It is not the sort of thing anyone can put to the test, but I feel there is a complex truth in this claim. That maleness is often felt as a kind of isolation, an understanding of the indifference of the world to your very existence.

Male isolation is in fact often encouraged by a broader culture that positions the individual man as a totemic, untouchable being for whom the world is a hostile place, with no succour. We can see this totem celebrated with violence in first-person shooter games, and we are the heirs of an entire literary tradition that portrays the individual man against his age, his family, his friends (if he has any) and against even his own mind. In existentialist literature, in particular Sartre's *Nausea* and Camus's *The Outsider*, we are presented with thinking men, who, when they act, act unbearably, who cannot cope with the expectations of the world, who cannot manage existence, who feel sick and alone and alien. We have become accustomed to imagining that the man who thinks, thinks alone.

This unbearable loneliness imagined as the precondition for both thought (in novels) and action (in computer games) generates a rather isolated image in the twentieth and twenty-first century of what it means to be a man. If this same culture promotes the idea that the reward for being this kind of man is a woman, we must ask ourselves what happens to and for those men for whom there is no woman or for whom women are not enough. And what, too, of the women who do not live up to their supposed role?

To discuss men's relation to suicide is to raise difficult questions. Questions concerning honour, status and pride, but also issues of care and protection. If male friendship is tied up only with valour and competition rather than vulnerability, any discussion of bleak feelings becomes impossible. For men to appear in need of help, it is necessary for them, paradoxically, to be strong enough to ask for it. Feeling anxious or depressed is still all too often perceived as embarrassing or shameful.

The seventeenth-century philosopher Spinoza suggests that suicide comes only from the outside, that is to say when one's own desire to persist is overwhelmed by too many negative forces. For anyone to recognize which forces are negative or positive, they must be able to describe them, in the first place, to a person or people they can trust. This possibility of a dialogue or a discussion about how one is feeling need not only be with a member of the same sex, yet perhaps there are things that are more easily understood among men.

The history of suicide is not an obvious or easy one to recount. Of course, there are more or less collective and individual ways of thinking about this act. There are more or less religious and literary ways of understanding this kind of action – or perhaps rather than as an 'action' it is better described as the feeling that one is overwhelmed by one's world.

Men today are subject to a series of contradictory instructions: they are told to take charge, to be responsible, to show initiative; but at the same time warned that their version of masculinity might be exhibiting privilege, or even be toxic. To encourage independence without support, to make every man an island, to make him solely responsible for everything that happens to him, is to create an anxious being for whom any missteps, social or sexual, are minefields. Indeed, today we could say that in the relationship between the sexes lies a kind of no man's land where few dare to tread for fear of being blown up or shot by the other side.

To be brave enough not only to talk to one's fellow man or woman about the anxiety that one might be suffering, but to move forward not knowing who might stand beside you, is always a risk. What if talking about these things was also understood to be another serious game? The king in chess has to be protected at all costs, and very little movement is available to him despite, or perhaps because, he is the bearer of ultimate meaning. And this is a great and terrible responsibility, for both men and women. But there is so much to live for: life is very surprising. It is worth sticking around just to see what might happen, if nothing else. And you never know who can help you when you're down: that too is sometimes amazing.

6.   What *Do* Men Want?

Men, we might say with a cheeky smile, are people too. They seem to want things, even if *what* they want is unclear – as it is, most of the time, for all of us. What does the contemporary world tell us men want? Domination, perhaps . . . *a penthouse flat, a big watch, a helicopter, some whiskey, gazing out of a massive window onto a desolate city where all human misery unfolds and the eternal emptiness of being is revealed in the minimal distance between the reflection of his stubbled jawline in expensive glass and the inner feeling of acute empty majesty* . . . this is a version of today's high-end consumerist image of masculinity, used to sell all those things that point to a coiled, modern tiger, a kind of lonely, isolationist manliness. But who is this man standing before us, beyond some sort of cinematic *noir*-meets-property-values fantasy? Do either men or women really want him – to have him or to be him? Does *he* even want his own life? Take away the building, the accessories, the clothes, the economic system and standing before us is *who* exactly . . . ?

When we talk about 'men', we don't necessarily have a clear conception of who or what we mean. We are in the realm of fantasy. Men are like the air we breathe. When we hear the word, we probably think of particular men – a father, brother, husband, son or boyfriend, or we might think of masculinity, of groups of men, of maleness or of the sexual act. We might throw up our hands in mock or actual despair – 'Men!' – or we might feel very little, a neutral sentiment.

When we see signs repeatedly, though, particularly if they have a negative association, we start to feel that they are no longer descriptive but rather carry the negative weight in themselves.

When we are told today that 'men are bad', we should pause to reflect – really? If they are, we should ask, what made them 'bad', and how do we change the situation? If our experience leads us to conclude this is not true, or at least that there are 'bad' and 'good' men, or that everyone is a mixture of good and bad, and we can all be better, we might further and critically ask: who wants us to think that men are bad? Why do they want us to think this?

We might, in everyday life, be wildly indifferent to the sex of the person we are serving, being served by, working with or passing by on the pavement. At the same time, we cannot fail to notice what sex someone is. We all have strong, if obscure, feelings about our sex and that of others, particularly when there are many other ways of understanding who we are – parent, or father, worker or unemployed, atheist or religious, left-wing or right-wing, and so on. In the current age – technological, consumerist, modern – we seem to be in the midst of a serious choice. Either we are an amorphous mass of bodies in which 'sex' as the defining feature of humanity disappears, or we might, consciously or unconsciously, continue to understand ourselves *in the first* place as individual members of two distinct groups.

In the aftermath of multiple waves of feminism, whose legacy in its current incarnation is perhaps more complicated than we imagine, post #MeToo, post the sensitive 'New Man' of the 1990s, where 'gender' has become another thing we can 'choose', where economies in the West depend in general less on physical strength than on basic literacy and numeracy, it has been suggested that men are 'over', somehow, as we saw above – that neither the economy nor culture has a need for men in their manliness. That men as a whole lack purpose and meaning.

I have tried to suggest that being a man today *could* instead be about being 'strong' again in various ways: courageous, kind, good, responsible, a reliable father. These are real choices. Real modes of behaviour. They are the opposite of avoiding life. How can men get back to reality?

No Dads

We live in an era without father figures, without older men to guide the younger. Perhaps there was never a truly 'golden age' of fathers, but we surely can imagine a better age than this one – it is hard to imagine how the role today could be any more evacuated of meaning or status. Young men are looking for dads. This desire explains the immense popularity of the afore-mentioned Canadian psychologist Jordan Peterson, author of *12 Rules for Life: An Antidote to Chaos* (2018). Peterson's popularity reveals that many young men strongly desire to improve their lives, and something about his paternalistic persona undoubt-edly appeals to them in their many thousands.

At base, Peterson's bestselling book presents a series of simple rules for improving one's lot: 'Stand up straight with your shoulders back', 'Treat yourself like someone you are respon-sible for helping' and 'Tell the truth – or, at least, don't lie'. 'We must have something to set against the suffering that is intrinsic to Being,' he writes. These patrician ideas of self-responsibility proved to be highly irresistible to people tired (*sick*, perhaps) of sitting in bedrooms looking for someone else to blame. If Jor-dan Peterson is a popular figure among young men in particular, it is in part because he presents an image and a reminder of a lost paternalism that combines concern with a kind of tough love and a paradoxical encouragement for autonomy.

There are those who laugh at the idea that something as basic as advising someone to tidy their room is in any way a useful thing to do, but the very fact that our culture requires it to be said is revealing, and in fact Peterson's advice has undeniably had some positive effects. Rather than accept state-sponsored infantilism, it suggests that a better way of living and of being admired is to take responsibility for oneself. Peterson's message that it is undesirable to remain stuck in an infantile position, that boys need to 'man up' if they hope to lead fulfilling lives, is good news for women too, even if many women would hardly see in Peterson a feminist hero. The more boys and men understand that they should not rely on women for their own care, and that women do not exist to provide men with attention, the more interesting (and interested) we will all be. Figures like Peterson, in presenting 'antidotes to chaos', are, even paradoxically, meeting a real desire on the part of both men and women.

There is something very human about wanting to emulate someone older and admirable. We all want someone to look up to. We all desire to listen to advice, to gain experience. Young people, all young people, know very little, though they might ask interesting questions and sometimes seek to become better people. Contemporary culture is a swirling mess of contradictory imperatives that often seem completely detached from the reality of young people's lives. They suffer from a culture that fetishizes them for their youth, even, or especially, when this youth is not well understood by them at the time to be any kind of great thing. We are all part of, and determined to some extent, by a culture that seems intent on keeping us down and immature, one way or another, through vast amounts of 'stuff', through competition. We are encouraged to be irresponsible.

When we do not take responsibility for ourselves or others, we are in fact demanding the right to remain as childlike as we can be. In this scenario, no one becomes a man or a woman, but rather everybody remains a perpetual infant or adolescent, even if they have children of their own. In a selfish and immature culture, we stop thinking carefully and reasonably, and our desires push their way to the front, to be met by an endless array of things to satisfy them. Virtues such as courage and patience are passed over or even mocked, as if someone who exhibits these qualities is somehow missing out on all the fun. Why wait to get married before having sex? You can meet someone on an app and hook up tonight! It is difficult to struggle against the modern world, and it is difficult to think for oneself, let alone for others.

In a childish culture it is easy to blame others for our own misfortunes. If we feel our life isn't going well, we can blame our parents, our last boyfriend or girlfriend, the opposite sex as a whole, the age we live in, or a small group of people (or lizards) running the world. It is not, of course, that there might not be good reason to 'blame' any, or all, of these individuals, groups or systems, but we can also grow up, become mature, take responsibility. When we look back upon our lives, it is unlikely that we will wish we had spent more time blaming others (or more time on our phones, for that matter). There is no doubt that, at the same time, we want harm to be recognized by others – both the harm that we have suffered and the harm that we ourselves have caused. Forgiveness must not be forgotten.

So what happens after blame and reckoning? The example of Roosh V, a celebrated (and reviled) pick-up artist, is strangely instructive here. In 2019, after many years of writing and touring, and publishing books such as *Game*, *Day Bang* and *Poosy Paradise*, Roosh, nearing forty, wrote:

> If you've been following my work for a while, you'll notice I've been warming up to faith in God over the years, especially the past year. This is due to witnessing the growth of evil in society, my personal experiences with unbridled hedonism, and my sister's death. This reached a climax when I received a message while on mushrooms which cemented that faith further.[1]

On his forum, where he has now banned discussion of 'fornica-
tion and pre-marital sexual activity' as well as 'pornographic or
vulgar language', Roosh outlines his personal development in
the following way, invoking the image of 'pills', as do many in
the online word of the manosphere:

> Blue pill: Ignorance, denial of nature
> Red pill: Truth through materialism (muscles, women, money,
> status)
> Black pill: Acceptance of one's powerlessness, withdrawal
> from materialist society
> God pill: Submission to God's will.[2]

What a curious turn-up for the books, we might think. A
pussy-seeking, one-night-stand kind of guy turning, finally, to
God. But perhaps it is not so strange if one asks the question,
what was it all for? All this questing after women, for 'pussy'. Just
for the numbers? The approval of his male friends? For status?
Clearly none of this was, in the end (or perhaps all along),
enough, for Roosh at least. After many years of pursuing
women, this man, who told many other men how to get women
to sleep with them, now turns to God the Father.

Roosh's story, and those of many others who have had some
kind of radical break or crisis in their life, demonstrates, among
other things, that transformation is possible. As the poet Rainer
Maria Rilke puts it in 'Archaic Torso of Apollo': 'you must
change your life'. Despite the consumerist, distracting confusion of 'life' as we are generally presented with it, there *are* better
and worse ways of living. There are better and worse ways of
being a man (or a woman). When we look for guidance we
want, sometimes desperately, to know what these are. As we
have seen, much of the literature in today's manosphere is dedicated to understanding what they might be.

Though we might mock self-help, there is nothing wrong

with aspiring to be better. We are today 'carefree', yet often excessively competitive, seeing in the other someone we dislike because we want to be them, or want what we think they have. This sibling society, with its job market and sexual market, presents men and women as rivals to each other and as rivals within their own sex too: if we want to look up to someone it is perhaps because we are tired of looking across and seeing our own worst qualities reflected back at us.

The post-war world is a mass society of atomic beings encouraged to be minutely better than the person next to them. When men and women begin to regard each other as proximate competitors in multiple markets what happens to the frisson of difference? Men and women are different and equal at the same time. Even if we want many of the same things – love, respect, recognition, enough money to live on – we live out our lives differently. We can learn to love and enjoy these differences, not pretend they don't exist.

We could spend our time on social media checking what the other thinks, and therefore what we should think. But this flattening out of desire into a battle of equality has nothing to do with real cooperation or solidarity. If we never look up towards the light, we find ourselves dragged into rabbit holes. And what happens when we don't like what we see? We come to regard our rival as an enemy. Societies before us, for better or worse, had a different relation to their ancestors, or at least *we believe they did*. Freud tells a famous story:

> One day the expelled brothers joined forces, slew and ate the father, and thus put an end to the father horde. Together they dared and accomplished what would have remained impossible for them singly. Perhaps some advance in culture, like the use of a new weapon, had given them the feeling of superiority. Of course these cannibalistic savages ate their victim. This

violent primal father had surely been the envied and feared model for each of the brothers. Now they accomplished their identification with him by devouring him and each acquired a part of his strength. The totem feast, which is perhaps mankind's first celebration, would be the repetition and commemoration of this memorable, criminal act with which so many things began, social organization, moral restrictions and religion.[3]

Freud's suggestion, as myth or otherwise, that we must kill the 'primal father' in order to establish him as the origin of law, points to a deep understanding of both fatherhood and the violent source of the rules of human society. Today, the myth of 'killing daddy in order to become daddy' belongs to an era that no longer exists. Despite claims that we live in or under patriarchy, we no longer live in a 'paternalistic' society. We are all somehow 'fatherless'.

It may be that we *had to* lose this world, that the father had to perish, so that something else could be born. So now there is (relative) equality between the sexes. Modern humanity has given up community, monarchy, sovereignty and tribalism in the name of progress. We no longer believe in wise men, in ritual, in sacrifice. We work to make money because we must, to keep the machine churning, to fill the time; levelling ourselves to meet the market, becoming the servant of capital.

We turn away from, among other things, a nature which much of work and consumption helps to destroy, and from a deeper conception of time, a more real understanding of love – and we are 'rewarded' in turn with superficial distractions and perhaps, if we are lucky, scattered glimpses of joy, a different way of living. We are no longer told 'what to do' by parents, husband, Church or tradition, and we may revel in our relative freedom, in our alienation, our infinite choices, our beautiful loneliness. But in this high-wire freedom it is imperative to wonder if we haven't in fact signed over our souls to new masters without faces, kindly or otherwise. The death of the father is not, in other words, the elimination of mastery or authority.[4]

Today paternalism is not only absent, but extensively vilified when it is understood to be merely another expression of patriarchy. The impossibility of imagining authority has meant that we've moved from a vertical relation to the father, who after all does not simply command but also protects and cares, to a society where Big Brother, or the Nanny State, is watching you. This brother (or sister) state is far less concerned with your well-being and your flourishing, and far more concerned with checking up and spying on you, in the name of a faceless, sexless, nameless power.

There are good fathers today. But where does this suspicion against their role come from? In the late 1960s and early 1970s, some revolutionary thinkers turned their sights on the family. Not for the first time, in fact, as many early Marxists and feminists had also described the forms of oppression and violence perpetuated by this institution. In the early 1970s psychologist and writer David Cooper, who coined the term 'anti-psychiatry', was interested in how the medical establishment dealt with mental illness, particularly what was at the time called 'schizophrenia'. The nuclear family, he suggested, reinforced the ruling class in an exploitative society, and he proposed that the family itself be abolished:

> it is fatuous to speak of the death of God or the death of Man – parodying the serious intent of certain contemporary theologians and structuralist philosophers – until we can fully envisage *the death of the family* – that system which, as its social obligation, obscurely filters out most of our experience and then deprives our acts of any genuine and generous spontaneity.[5]

Cooper's criticism of the family is of an institution that inhibits us from attaining real experience, that conditions our acts and feelings and thoughts; he suggests that in order to move past these kinds of restrictions and oppressions, we should collectively engage in a kind of 'summing up' of our family past 'so as to be free of it'.

But while we might be able to positively change our attitude to family, or lack of family, it is not clear that we as a society have managed to yet 'go beyond' the family, as such, nor indeed that most people particularly want to. Today people create alternative social arrangements, and others imagine technological routes into a post-family era, but the family remains strong everywhere we look. Rather than see it as a repetition and reinforcement of state and capitalist exploitation, we might also, as Marx partly did, see it as a 'haven'. I don't think the family is going anywhere: much of the time, in fact, we love our families. We should collectively be able to trust that families have each other's best interests at heart and work to support our friends and people we know when we suspect that this is not the case for them. This requires courage.

Alongside the necessary bringing to awareness of the violence sometimes shielded by the nuclear family, one of the major trickle-down successes of second-wave feminism was also to make it clear that fatherhood did not need to be a distant thing, and that caring for children can be a shared and joyful enterprise. Many men today indeed seek to be great and present fathers. There are also some leaders who seek to step into the place of the father. Think of Vladimir Putin and Donald Trump, among others, who combine authority with a certain macho, or even clownish, quality (I have a mug with Putin riding a bear and Trump holding a gun and riding a lion that a friend brought back from Russia). These men revel in certain aspects of masculinity, often to much disgust, as in Trump's infamous comment regarding 'grabbing' women 'by the pussy'. But, given the popularity of these kinds of men in some places, we have to ask ourselves, what need are they responding to? Why do people vote for strong-seeming men?

Part of the answer to the question 'what do men want?' might well be: to *have* and to *be* fathers, where the definition of this term includes but goes beyond its biological meaning towards something approaching goodness – the stern but kind father, the father who knows things, who passes on wisdom. There are ways of relating to our own desire to have and to be the father, regardless of whether we are men or women, that are more or less subtle. The father, actual, social, remains a permanent part of our being.[6] And yet we are often encouraged to pretend we are beyond fathers, in no need of boundaries, care, direction, protection: we are all individuals, unbounded by anything that might get in the way of our pleasure or particular identity.

Our sibling society tells men and women to compete at the level of employment and sex, among other things. The 'ladette' culture I mentioned in the Introduction was a part of this tendency: the idea that young women could be as hedonistic as we imagined young men to be. There is a kind of equality in behaving excessively that strives to compete with a certain idea of masculinity, even where this behaviour is hardly that of all young men (there are obviously quiet men, and men who do not drink alcohol). Men and women nevertheless are increasingly behaving in the same way. We do the same kinds of jobs, we live heterosocially: in the contemporary West, the other sex is perhaps less of a mystery than before. To sense the desire of the other up close is, in this respect, sometimes off-putting. This proximate cocktail of infantilism and horizontalism is part of an ongoing attack and destruction of positive, older modes of being together. No wonder resentment is such common currency.

It is often said that there are not enough male role models, particularly in primary schools and in family settings, the absence of which has had a particularly negative impact on young men. There is a widespread absence of father-led upbringings which would both guide and ultimately liberate, however painful this liberation might be. The idea of men instructing or mentoring younger men is often greeted with suspicion about the possibilities for abuse of this role. But in our understandable desire to protect young boys and girls from those who would seek to hurt them, we also and too quickly undermine the possibility of genuinely kind, caring and informative intergenerational relationships.

In the absence of male guides or mentors a space is opened up for other kinds of manipulation. Only now this brainwashing comes less from individual men but rather from faceless systems whose rules and punishments stem not from care but from pathological bureaucracy and top-down control of the masses.

Good Men

Contemporary culture attempts to convince us that we have transcended the need for older virtues such as temperance, stoicism, self-control or loyalty. Why be a good person when you can, in principle and in a day, buy twelve different cakes, eat them all, then dump an old friend on a whim after they suggest that your behaviour might not be ideal, knowing that you can pick up a new mate or pal via an app, and even buy some more cake later? There is no limit to the absurd and self-destructive behaviour that capitalism permits, all the while telling you that this is the best you've ever had it, and that this is what you want. But some of the older virtues, particularly those most associated with men, might be precisely what we all need today.

Capitalism encourages a lack of self-restraint, a kind of

perpetual toddler-like demand for things, along with the idea that people are also 'things'. Imagine instead a world of adults, men and women both, who take responsibility for themselves and each other, who treat each other with care and not as disposable accessories to a selfish life. We should be extremely wary of anyone selling us the kind of life that involves *indifference* to each other, whether it be an existence that privileges sex but not sex with *somebody*, or a culture that suggests that the best way to deal with difficult emotions such as regret, sadness and anger, is to look outside for an explanation rather than seeking to analyse one's own thoughts and feelings first. *Caveat emptor* is a slogan for consumer goods, not human beings. This is not to suggest that people, and especially some men when it comes to violence of various kinds, do not do terrible things – they do – but that a world in which one sex is blamed for all the ills of the world is a dangerous one. It implies that there are pure victims and pure villains, which is never, for adults at least, true. True equality means accepting that life is hard. That everyone must – eventually – take responsibility for their actions, the better to live together and to flourish.

Our experience of being a sexed being, and the way in which our sex is lived out, is shaped from birth (or even before). Yet we often barely know who we are, let alone what we want, or whether that wanting comes from within or from without. Leaving aside larger existential and philosophical questions – why are we here? What is the purpose of life? – we can focus on what it is we seem to desire in the here and now.

Naturally, asking the question of what men today want is a question of guesswork – a dream, or a game, in which we can isolate a core desire or set of desires, as if these things exist in a pure state, beyond other factors. Yet, on the other hand, why *not* ask this kind of question? Men have for a long time speculated on what it is that women *want*, and bemoaned as well as celebrated the 'mystery' of women and femininity. Women are insanely obscure creatures! men cried. They must be either extremely good or extremely evil and must be rescued or denounced, or sometimes both ... Why not, when men and masculinity once more seem to be under attack and in a confused state, ask the same question of our male counterparts?

Our sex is something *nobody* can be neutral towards. There is no third position on sex, no alien-like observatory to gaze out from or bird's-eye view to adopt. Women, myself included, cannot know exactly what it is like to be a man, nor do we have direct access to this thing called 'male desire', let alone feel the variety and range of this desire: how could we?

Yet the world is shared: we are none of us an island, and there are signs and symbols everywhere, clues as to what might be going on in broad terms. None of us has access to anyone else's inner mental states, but someone's behaviour will tell us a lot of what we need to know: whether this man or woman is kind, hostile or indifferent, and what they are doing in the short term. But where does desire reside? Not only in our conscious life. We are used, after Freud, to thinking about what we 'really' want as being partially hidden, lurking iceberg-like beneath the surface of the every-man or -woman we imagine ourselves to be, and certainly distant from how we present ourselves to the world. We imagine that our desires are murky, possibly unpleasant, and certainly not something fit for social or public investigation. We often do not know how to access them, though there are many psychological snake-oil salespeople offering to 'unlock' them in various ways. Yet it turns out we can and should do this work ourselves, with a little patience. In the end, there's really no way around this.

Men and women each seem to the other to promise a solution to the riddle of meaning: if I understand the opposite sex, or this particular embodiment of the opposite sex, will my life finally make sense? The romantic ideal thrives still, despite, or perhaps because of, in the West, declining marriage rates. So much weight is placed on the need for *an other* to make sense of our life, to give meaning to our existence. The relatively recent freedom to choose a partner has generated a whole host of new issues, which can perhaps be boiled down to one question: how can I be sure this one person will give my life the meaning I am after? Men, just as much as women, are looking for sense, though they are usually positioned as the one who provides purpose rather than the one who receives it. But who really knows what's going on? Quite possibly no one, really, but it is wonderful to try to find a companion in absurdity.

Rather than passively receiving meaning from the culture that surrounds us, which in any case is a confusing amalgam of conflicting demands and desires, we know, as the existentialists did, that we must make our own meaning if there is to be any sense at all. This meaning might come from tradition, from family, from ritual, from older ways of doing things. Why not? During the twentieth century, people seemed to demand the free flow of desire. Yet unleashed and unchecked libidinal energy, a kind of generalized id, is detrimental to society as a whole. We do not, on reflection, actually want to live in a world in which competing adult sexual desires dominate the social or political sphere. Private life is called that for a reason. Repression has its advantages.

History is often described in a progressive way: things are getting better because *they must be* getting better, because things just 'get better', don't they? The desire to be 'on the right side of history' is a deeply human need, and we all want to believe our age is the most advanced yet. We think that our sexual and emotional relationships must have reached some kind of great peak of complexity from which we can survey and understand everything that our ancestors somehow did not. There is 'liberation' from what we imagine are the superstitions of the past. But everyone is linked to all the dead and the living in myriad and strange ways. The dead do not stop being right about how to live just because they are no longer among us.

If we instead conceive of time not as a purchase against the future in which the other is a kind of investment, but rather as a perpetual and joyful present, we might start to understand and love each other better. Think of a relationship with someone you love where you did not know for sure if you would see them again the next day. Imagine what a heightened mode of being together this would induce. No more taking the other for granted, treating them as if they were simply some sort of warm body-pillow to watch TV with, but rather a unique, poetic and strange person whom one happens to find oneself next to. What a magical way of relating this would be! If we did not regard each other as comfort animals, but rather as companions in the infinite, life would be so much more extraordinary.

This would require changing our understanding of time. Time and sexual difference would take on a different meaning in which we could 'live for ever' alongside the other by virtue of seeing in them the infinite possibilities generated by together-ness. This does not have to be limited only to erotic romantic relationships between men and women; friendship between men and men, and between women and women, can occupy this kind of reality too. Time with our families can also be like this. Beyond work, our only real decision could be who, at any moment, we might wish to spend time with, without feeling anxious for the future, nostalgic for the past, or pressure to be anywhere else. This doesn't mean that we don't have responsi-bilities to our friends, partners and families: in fact, it means precisely this. We must often (and should) do things for others in the name of care, duty and love.

So, what *do* men want? To live, like everyone. For their lives to mean something – to themselves, to others. Contemporary culture seems to offer largely sibling rivalry and useless objects. Yet we can decide to live instead with a mature yet light-hearted acceptance of our responsibilities, and to dignify our lives, minds and bodies to the best of our ability. We can accept our role in a vision of the world and history that links old with new, men with women, fathers with mothers, children with adults, and individuals with humanity as a whole.

In the first place, men can take responsibility for their desire *as* men. They can avoid blaming women for failures and any lack they might feel: women can equally avoid blaming men. Sometimes a bad relationship was just that – no one was totally in the right or in the wrong. Most relationships break down through no one's fault in particular. To generalize negatively from a bad experience with one person is to limit your future vision of the world. No one is perfect. Everyone makes mistakes, and there's always room for improvement. We need to collectively stand up against a culture of fear and punishment, and not to back down in the face of hypothetical online denunciations. When we talk to each other face to face things are much less simple, in a good way. Even if we don't agree, or want never to see each other again, we can do all that bravely, as adults. We can be self-aware, responsible, courageous and in control of our life. We can try to be good.

Conclusion: Forgiveness and Reconciliation

'I suppose that you're half victim and half
accomplice, like everybody else'

Hoederer in *Dirty Hands* by Jean-Paul Sartre[1]

I want to end by suggesting that the time is right for an attempt
at a general reconciliation between men and women. This aim
may of course turn out to be naive, if not simply impossible.
How can it be remotely possible to square political and ideological positions that prioritize one sex over the other?
Nevertheless, this is the dream, for better or for worse.

To understand existing resentments between the sexes doesn't
preclude the possibility of overcoming them. As social psychologist Roy F. Baumeister puts it: 'It would be better for men
and women to appreciate each other's contributions more. Men
and women have been partners throughout human history,
mostly working together for the good of both ... A bit of
mutual gratitude would be quite appropriate.'[2] We all have different strengths: if some lie more with men than women, and
vice versa, then so be it. To be different is not to be worse: we
can value all of our different aptitudes and ambitions. Life would
be intensely horrible and boring if we all did and thought the
same thing. If some women want to work, great. If some want
to raise children at home, great. The same goes for men too!

We are often told that there is a divide between what men
want and what women want, and nowhere more so than in their

relations with one another. By analysing the image of the world
presented by guidebooks and literature aimed at men, it is possible
to let women know how life is understood by men. Some of it is
certainly revealing, and parts of it are not particularly pleasant.

Criticism of men as a class in recent years indicates a boiling-
over of long-held grievances that can barely be contained.
Similarly, when some men engage in unbridled women-hatred
online and off, and/or regard women as mysterious, and possibly slightly dangerous creatures to be held at arm's length, we
might continue to wonder how such distance can be bridged.

At first glance, it seems ludicrous to propose that there are more
points of similarity than difference between extreme masculinist
movements and feminism – after all, how can patriarchy-deniers
talk to patriarchy-believers? In recent decades the discussion of
men, women, masculinity and femininity has oscillated wildly
between deep essentialism ('men are or should be like this'; 'women
are or should be like this') and extreme social construction (men
and women are not biological realities, and masculinity, femininity, neither or both, are floating options).

Yet we know that life is not all just a grim war of the sexes.
Sometimes – hopefully often! – there is joyful complicity, affection, laughter, friendship and love. It may be the case for now
that certain negative ways of seeing the world have become
dominant on both the masculinist and the feminist side, and we
must tread carefully for fear of skimming over genuine frustration and hurt. Hopefully, though, we can at the same time think
beyond various stalemates, misconceptions and misunderstandings and ask not only what it is that men want, but also what it
is that women want, and, furthermore, what it is that men and
women want *together*, whether as friends or as partners. It is easy,
unfortunately, to do nothing but hate, resent and blame. It is
much harder to be both an adult and playful, and accept high
levels of rejection, suffering, beauty and uncertainty.

It is courageous to recognize one's own flaws and nevertheless seek to go beyond them to improve oneself, mentally, physically and imaginatively. Many of the positive images and texts of masculinity today push this point, not necessarily with a view to providing heterosexual men with a better basis to form or maintain relationships with women, but often just to improve their lives and their friendships with other men, and this is a good thing.

Nowadays marriage and cohabitation are only just about more dominant than solitary existence, so we might ask, what future for men and women? We have as men and women lived under the banner of 'sexual liberation' for almost sixty years now, but what has it led to? If one of our major contemporary fears is a return to conservative values, involving arranged marriages, a lack of reproductive choice and stereotypical gender roles, we nevertheless must ask ourselves some difficult questions. What has sexual liberation done for (or to) us, men and women alike? As we have seen, sex, like money or good looks, is not fairly distributed. Suffering is a fact of life, but we are all tougher than we think we are. We never know what life may bring. It is important, even in the depths of despair, not to give up. You cannot imagine who you might meet or what life may bring. The sky belongs to all of us.

I want to end this brief tour of men by noting that the *way* that men and women talk to each other is as important as *what* they say, and that what they say about each other is also a way of speaking about themselves. A speaking culture must also be a listening culture. What might we hear if we pay attention? Men and women work very well together – to return to my opening axiom: none of us would be here if we didn't.

This book may be interpreted by some as a conservative analysis of men and women, and if it is read in this way that cannot be helped. Not everything that our ancestors understood is irrelevant, and not everything new is good. On the contrary. We would do well to revisit old values and virtues – honour, loyalty, courage – in the name of reconciliation. The games we play as men and women, separately and together, are cosmic, and all of our lives are meaningful, even when they seem bleak and sad. To imagine that men and women can be better, and are fated most wonderfully to sometimes be together, is, in the end, to respect the strange marvel of human existence as a whole.

Acknowledgements

I would like to thank Helen Conford, who originally commissioned me to write this book. I would also very much like to thank Maria Bedford, who has been an excellent editor. My thanks also to Matthew Hamilton at The Hamilton Agency.

I would like to thank, without naming them individually here, all the men and women who spoke to me about this book, and those who commented on the manuscript. I'm also grateful to all those who invited me to speak about masculinity during the writing of this book, including Peter Limberg at The Stoa and Henk de Berg at the University of Sheffield.

Notes

Introduction

1 Kathleen Stock, *Material Girls: Why Reality Matters for Feminism* (London: Fleet, 2021), p. 7.

2 Jack Grove, 'Kathleen Stock: Life on the Front Lines of Transgender Rights Debate', *Times Higher Education*, 7 January 2020. Available at https://www.timeshighereducation.com/news/kathleen-stock-life-front-line-transgender-rights-debate

3 Pauline Harmange, *I Hate Men*, translated by Natasha Lehrer (London: 4th Estate, 2020), p. 4.

4 Ibid., p. 5.

5 Hanna Rosin, 'The End of Men', *Atlantic*, July/August 2010. Available at https://www.theatlantic.com/magazine/archive/2010/07/the-end-of-men/308135/

6 Nina Power, *One-Dimensional Woman* (Winchester: Zero Books, 2009).

7 Massimo Recalcati, *In Praise of Forgiveness*, trans. Alice Kilgarriff (Cambridge: Polity Press, 2020), pp. 116–17.

8 Raven Connolly described this idea of hers to me originally.

9 Ivan Illich, *Tools for Conviviality* (London: Calder & Boyars, 1973), p. xiii.

10 Aldous Huxley, *Brave New World* (London: Penguin Books, 1974), p. 187.

1. *Modern Man in Search of a Role*

1 Jack@ofwhichnothing, Twitter, 12 December 2020. Available at https://twitter.com/ofwhichnothing/status/133770994726666 6497

2 Judith N. Shklar, *Ordinary Vices* (Cambridge, Massachusetts & London: The Belknap Press of Harvard University Press, 1984), pp. 18–19.

3 Jordan Peterson, *12 Rules for Life: An Antidote to Chaos* (London: Allen Lane, 2018), p. 27.

4 Ed West, 'Wanted: A Female Jordan Peterson', *UnHerd*, 9 December 2020. Available at https://unherd.com/thepost/wanted-a-female-jordan-peterson/

5 Mary Harrington, Twitter, 10 December 2020. Available at https://twitter.com/moveincircles/status/1336937887661744129

6 Mary Harrington, Twitter, 10 December 2020. Available at https://twitter.com/moveincircles/status/1336937891197546496

7 Maya Salem, *The New York Times*, 22 January 2019. Available at https://www.nytimes.com/2019/01/22/us/toxic-masculinity.html

8 Lara Rutherford-Morrison, '6 Subtle Mansplanations Women Encounter Everyday', *Bustle*, 19 January 2016. Available at https://www.bustle.com/articles/136319-6-subtle-forms-of-mansplaining-that-women-encounter-each-day

9 Van Badham, '"Mentrification": How Men Appropriated Computers, Beer and the Beatles', *Guardian*, 28 May 2019. Available at https://www.theguardian.com/music/2019/may/29/mentrification-how-men-appropriated-computers-beer-and-the-beatles

10 Harris O'Malley, 'Treating Men Like Idiots Is the Wrong Way to Stop Sexual Harassment', *Washington Post*, 2 February 2018. Available at https://www.washingtonpost.com/news/post-nation/wp/2018/02/01/for-men-in-the-metoo-era-the-mike-pence-rule-is-the-easy-way-out/

11 Sylvia Ann Hewlett, 'Threatened by Scandal, Women Need Support', *Harvard Business Review*, 15 September 2010. Available at https://hbr.org/2010/09/threatened-by-scandal-women-ne

12 'Full Translation of French Anti-#Me Too Manifesto Signed by Catherine Deneuve', *Worldcrunch*, 10 January 2018 (originally published in *Le Monde*). Available at https://www.worldcrunch.com/opinion-analysis/full-translation-of-french-anti-metoo-manifesto-signed-by-catherine-deneuve

13 The woman, known only by her first name, Alana, coined the term more than two decades ago. The origin of the word is discussed in 'The "Incel" Community and the Dark Side of the Internet' by Justin Ling, Jill Mahoney, Patrick McGuire and Colin Freeze, *Globe and Mail*, 24 April 2018. Available at https://www.theglobeandmail.com/canada/article-the-incel-community-and-the-dark-side-of-the-internet/

14 Kate Manne, *Entitled: How Male Privilege Hurts Women* (London: Allen Lane, 2020), p. 18.

15 Leana S. Wen and Nakisa B. Sadeghi, 'The Opioid Crisis and the 2020 US Election: Crossroads for a National Epidemic', *Lancet*, 6 October 2020. Available at https://www.thelancet.com/journals/lancet/article/PIIS0140-6736(20)32113-9/fulltext

16 Grayson Perry, *The Descent of Man* (London: Allen Lane, 2017), p. 2.

17 American Psychological Association, Boys and Men Guidelines Group, *APA Guidelines for Psychological Practice with Boys and Men* (2018). Available at http://www.apa.org/about/policy/psychological-practice-boys-men-guidelines.pdf

18 Ibid.

19 Ibid.

20 The Editors, 'The New Science of Sex and Gender', *Scientific American*, 1 September 2017. Available at https://www.scientificamerican.com/article/the-new-science-of-sex-and-gender/

21 Colin Wright, 'JK Rowling Is Right – Sex Is Real and It Is Not a "Spectrum"', *Quillette*, 7 June 2020. Available at https://quillette.

com/2020/06/07/jk-rowling-is-right-sex-is-real-and-it-is-not-a-spectrum/

22 Janice Turner, 'Keira Bell: I couldn't sit by while so many others made the same mistake', *The Times*, 1 December 2020. Available at https://www.thetimes.co.uk/article/keira-bell-i-couldnt-sit-by-while-so-many-others-made-the-same-mistake-gb03n3mlr

23 Jean-Jacques Courtine, 'Brawn in Civilization', in *A History of Virility*, ed. Alain Corbin, Jean-Jacques Courtine, Georges Vigarello, trans. Keith Cohen (New York: Columbia University Press, 2017), p. 587.

24 John Carlin, 'What Do Men Really Want?', *Independent*, 3 August 1997. Available at https://www.independent.co.uk/news/what-do-men-really-want-1243593.html

25 Christopher Lasch, *The Culture of Narcissism: American Life in an Age of Diminishing Expectations* (New York: W. W. Norton, 1991), p. 189.

26 Ibid.

27 Ibid., p. 191.

28 Ibid., p. 205.

29 Ibid., p. 206.

30 Ibid.

31 Both figures include marriage/cohabitation with a person of the opposite sex or the same sex, the latter of which was legalized in the UK from 2014. See May Bulman, 'Marriages Between Men and Women Hit Lowest Rate on Record', *Independent*, 28 February 2018. Available at https://www.independent.co.uk/news/uk/home-news/marriages-men-women-lowest-record-heterosexual-lgbt-ons-a8232751.html. Also Office for National Statistics, *Population Estimates by Marital Status and Living Arrangements, England and Wales: 2002 to 2017*, 27 July 2018. Available at https://www.ons.gov.uk/peoplepopulationandcommunity/populationandmigration/populationestimates/bulletins/populationestimatesbymaritalstatusandlivingarrangements/2002to2017

2. What is the Patriarchy?

1 Mary Daly, *Gyn/Ecology: The Metaethics of Radical Feminism* (Boston: Beacon Press, 1978), Introduction.

2 bell hooks, *The Will to Change: Men, Masculinity, and Love* (New York: Washington Square Press, 2004).

3 Alexander Mitscherlich, *Society without the Father: A Contribution to Social Psychology*, trans. Eric Mosbacher (New York: Tavistock Publications, 1969).

4 Alex Gendler, 'The New Superfluous Men', *American Affairs* IV:4 (Winter 2020), pp. 179–87. Available at https://american affairsjournal.org/2020/11/the-new-superfluous-men/

5 Arizona State University Project Humanities, 'Male Privilege Checklist'. Available at https://projecthumanities.asu.edu/content/male-privilege-checklist

6 Ellie Mae O'Hagan, 'I Love Swimming, but I'm Sick of the Sexist Behaviour in British Pools', *Guardian*, 7 May 2019. Available at https://www.theguardian.com/commentisfree/2019/may/07/swimming-sexist-behaviour-british-pools-male-swimmers-men

7 Jean Baudrillard, *Seduction*, trans. Bryan Singer (Montréal: New World Perspectives, 1990), p. 2.

8 Jean Baudrillard, 'Afterword: *Amor Fati* (a Letter from Baudrillard)', in *Baudrillard Live: Selected Interviews*, ed. Mike Gane, trans. G. Salemohamed and M. Gane, (London: Routledge, 1993), p. 209.

9 Camille Paglia, *Free Women, Free Men: Sex, Gender, Feminism* (Edinburgh: Canongate Books, 2017), p. 132.

10 1 April 2021. Available at https://www.psychologytoday.com/gb/blog/culture-conscious/202104/why-do-men-have-the-most-dangerous-jobs

11 Health and Safety Executive, *Workplace Fatal Injuries in Great Britain, 2020*, 1 July 2020. Available at http://www.hse.gov.uk/statistics/pdf/fatalinjuries.pdf

12 Yanna J. Weisberg, Colin G. DeYoung and Jacob B. Hirsh, 'Gender differences in personality across the ten aspects of the Big Five', *Frontiers in Psychology*, 1 August 2011.

13 Meghan Murphy, 'Are we women or are we menstruators?', *Feminist Current*, 7 September 2016. Available at https://www.feministcurrent.com/2016/09/07/are-we-women-or-are-we-men struators/

14 Geoffrey Miller, Twitter, 9 August 2018. Available at https://twitter.com/primalpoly/status/1027377933260742658

15 United Nations Office on Drugs and Crime, *Global Study on Homicide*, UNODC Homicide statistics 2013. Available at https://www.unodc.org/gsh/en/data.html

16 UN Women, 'Facts and Figures: Ending Violence Against Women', November 2020. Available at http://www.unwomen.org/en/what-we-do/ending-violence-against-women/facts-and-figures

17 https://twitter.com/Ugly87925233 (since deleted).

18 Ezra Klein, 'The Problem with Twitter as Shown by the Sarah Jeong Fracas', *Vox*, 8 August 2018. Available at https://www.vox.com/technology/2018/8/8/17661368/sarah-jeong-twitter-new-york-times-andrew-sullivan

19 Valerie Solanas, *SCUM Manifesto* (San Francisco: AK Press, 1996).

20 Richard Partington, 'If it was Lehman Sisters it would be a different world', *Guardian*, 5 September 2018. Available at https://www.theguardian.com/business/2018/sep/05/if-it-was-lehman-sisters-it-would-be-a-different-world-christine-lagarde

21 Rahav Gabay, Boaz Hameiri, Tammy Rubel-Lifschitz and Arie Nadler, 'The tendency for interpersonal victimhood: The personality construct and its consequences', *Personality and Individual Differences*, Volume 165, 15 October 2020.

22 Ibid., p. 1.

23 Katherine Timpf, 'Netflix Bans Employees from Looking at Each Other for More Than Five Seconds', *National Review*, 14 June 2018.

Available at https://www.nationalreview.com/2018/06/netflix-five-second-staring-rule/

24 See Michael R. Kauth, 'The Changing Climate of Friendship', *Baylor College of Medicine*, 24 June 2021. Available at https://blogs.bcm.edu/2021/04/09/the-changing-climate-of-friendship/

25 Joanna Pepin and David Cotter, 'Trending Towards Traditionalism? Changes in Youths' Gender Ideology', *Council on Contemporary Families*, 30 March 2017. Available at https://contemporaryfamilies.org/2-pepin-cotter-traditionalism/

26 Louise Perry, 'What Sort of Sex Do Woman Really Want?', *UnHerd*, 1 April 2020. Available at https://unherd.com/2020/04/what-sort-of-sex-do-women-really-want/

27 Jean Baudrillard, 'After the Orgy', *The Transparency of Evil : Essays on Extreme Phenomena*, trans. James Benedict (London: Verso, 1993), p. 3.

28 Paul Elam, *Men. Women. Relationships: Surviving the Plague of Modern Masculinity* (self-published, 2019), Kindle edition.

3. Is Masculinity the Problem?

1 Nick Bostrom, 'Transhumanist Values', *Ethical Issues for the 21st Century*, ed. Frederick Adams (Philosophical Documentation Center Press, 2003). Available at https://www.nickbostrom.com/ethics/values.html

2 Grayson Perry, *The Descent of Man* (London: Allen Lane, 2017), p. 2.

3 Ibid., p. 3.

4 Robert Webb, *How Not to Be a Boy* (Edinburgh: Canongate Books, 2017), p. 325.

5 Campaign Against Living Miserably (CALM), 'Get Help On: Suicidal Thoughts'. Available at https://www.thecalmzone.net/help/get-help/suicide/

6 Office for National Statistics, *Suicides in the UK: 2017 Registrations*, 4 September 2018. Available at https://www.ons.gov.uk/people populationandcommunity/birthsdeathsandmarriages/deaths/bull etins/suicidesintheunitedkingdom/2017registrations

7 Denis Campbell, 'Cancer Risk Much Greater Among Men', *Guardian*, 29 January 2013. Available at https://www.theguardian. com/society/2013/jan/29/men-cancer-deaths-greater-women

8 Glen Poole, 'Homelessness Is a Gendered Issue, and It Mostly Impacts Men', *Telegraph*, 6 August 2015. Available at https://www. telegraph.co.uk/men/thinking-man/11787304/Homelessness-is-a-gendered-issue-and-it-mostly-impacts-men.html

9 Glen Poole, 'Nine Out of Ten Victims of Police-Related Deaths Are Male. Who Cares?', *Inside Man*, 24 July 2015. Available at http://www.inside-man.co.uk/2015/07/24/nine-out-of-ten-victims-of-police-related-deaths-are-male-who-cares/

10 Office for National Statistics, *The Nature of Violent Crime in England and Wales: Year Ending March 2017*, 8 February 2018. Available at https://www.ons.gov.uk/peoplepopulationandcommunity/crime andjustice/articles/thenatureofviolentcrimeinenglandandwales/ yearendingmarch2017

11 Fathers4Justice, 'Fact Sheet: The Key Facts About Family Break-down and Fatherlessness in the UK'. Available at https://www. fathers-4-justice.org/about-f4j/fact-sheet/

12 Office for National Statistics, *Homicide in England and Wales: Year Ending March 2018*, 7 February 2019. Available at https://www. ons.gov.uk/peoplepopulationandcommunity/crimeandjustice/ articles/homicideinenglandandwales/yearendingmarch2018# how-are-victims-and-suspects-related

13 N. Quentin Woolf, 'Our Attitude to Violence Against Men is Out of Date', *Telegraph*, 9 April 2014. Available at https://www. telegraph.co.uk/men/thinking-man/10752232/Our-attitude-to-violence-against-men-is-out-of-date.html

14 Rosalind Miles, *The Rites of Man: Love, Sex and Death in the Making of the Male* (London: Paladin, 1991), p. 8.

15 ManKind Initiative, 'Male Victims of Domestic and Partner Abuse: 35 Key Facts', March 2018. Available at https://www.man kind.org.uk/wp-content/uploads/2018/04/35-Key-Facts-Male-Victims-March-2018-1.pdf

16 Cordelia Fine, *Delusions of Gender: The Real Science Behind Sex Differences* (London: Faber & Faber, 2010), p. xxii.

17 Ibid., p. 7.

18 Phil Christman, 'What Is It Like to Be a Man?', *Hedgehog Review* 20:2 (Summer 2018). Available at https://hedgehogreview.com/issues/identitieswhat-are-they-good-for/articles/what-is-it-like-to-be-a-man

19 Ibid.

20 Ibid.

21 Claire Armistead, 'Feminism Was a Success, But Then You Lose a Generation', interview with Fay Weldon, *Guardian*, 31 March 2017. Available at https://www.theguardian.com/books/2017/mar/31/fay-weldon-interview-feminism-death-of-a-she-devil

22 Sigmund Freud, *Three Essays on the Theory of Sexuality: The 1905 Edition*, trans. Ulrike Kistner, ed. and intro. Philippe van Haute and Herman Westerink (London: Verso, 2016), Introduction, p. xl.

23 Sigmund Freud, 'Some Psychical Consequences of the Anatomical Distinction between the Sexes', Standard Edition 19 (London: Hogarth Press, 1961), p. 258.

24 James Bloodworth, 'Just how toxic is the masculine mystique?', *UnHerd*, 1 December 2020. Available at https://unherd.com/2020/12/just-how-toxic-is-the-masculine-mystique/

25 'Revisiting Jill Johnston's Critique of Robert Bly and "Iron John"', *The New York Times*, 2 August 2019.

26 Keith Thompson, '"What Men Really Want": A New Age Interview with Robert Bly', *New Age Journal* 84 (May 1982).

27 John A. Sanford, *The Invisible Partners: How the Male and Female in Each of Us Affects Our Relationships* (New York: Paulist Press, 1980), p. 3.

28 *Hermetis Trismegisti Tractatus vere Aureus* (1610), quoted ibid., with reference to Jung's letters.

29 Quoted in Thompson, 'What Men Really Want'.

30 Robert Bly, *Iron John: A Book About Men* (Reading, Massachusetts: Addison-Wesley Publishing Company, 1990), p. 6.

31 Ibid., p. 15.

32 Ibid., p. 16.

33 Ibid., p. 19.

34 Vic Seidler, 'Men, Sexual Politics and Socialism' in *The Achilles Heel Reader: Men, Sexual Politics & Socialism* (London: Routledge, 1991), p. 6.

35 Ole Bjerg, *The Meaning of Being a Man* (New York: Athos Press, 2020).

36 Ibid., p. 213.

37 Ryan Landry, *Masculinity Amidst Madness* (Terror House Press, 2020), pp. 1, 79, 106.

38 Hunter Drew, *31 Days to Masculinity: A Guide to Help Men Live Authentic Lives* (Create Space Independent Publishing Platform, 2017), Kindle edition.

39 P. D. Mangan Health and Fitness Maximalist, Twitter, 10 September 2018. Available at https://twitter.com/Mangan150/status/1039149602920747008

40 P. D. Mangan Health and Fitness Maximalist, Twitter, 10 June 2018. Available at https://twitter.com/Mangan150/status/1005597761616482305

41 Anne Dufourmantelle, *Power of Gentleness: Meditations on the Risk of Living*, trans. Katherine Payne and Vincent Sallé (New York: Fordham University Press, 2018), p. 25.

4. The Games Men Play

1 Online Etymology Dictionary, 'Game'. Available at https://www. etymonline.com/word/game#etymonline_v_1253

2 J. Huizinga, *Homo Ludens: A Study of the Play Element in Culture* (London: Routledge, 1949), p. 7.

3 Ibid., p. 19.

4 Ibid., p. 43.

5 'The Complete Maxims of Chateau Heartiste', Maxim #24. Available at https://gnosticwars.wordpress.com/2019/10/01/the-complete-maxims-of-chateau-heartiste/

6 Neil Strauss, *The Game: Penetrating the Secret Society of Pickup Artists* (New York: Harper Collins, 2005), p. 6.

7 Ibid., p. 9.

8 Ibid., p. 87.

9 LegalFling, https://legalfling.io/

10 Melanie Ehrenkranz, 'Men Try to Redefine Sexual Consent with Blockchain', *Gizmodo*, 10 January 2018. Available at https://gizmodo.com/men-try-to-redefine-sexual-consent-with-blockchain-1821964907

11 Elias Canetti, *Crowds and Power*, trans. Carol Stewart (Harmondsworth: Penguin, 1962), p. 15.

12 Aditi Johar Mirchandani, 'Smartphone Addiction, Social Media and Our Mental Health', *Thrive Global*, 22 January 2018. Available at https://medium.com/thrive-global/smartphone-addiction-social-media-and-our-mental-health-aditi-mirchandani-b2e9229bd0d8

13 Aamna Mohdin, 'No Touching: The Countries That Dislike Physical Contact the Most', *The Atlantic*, 29 October 2015. Available at https://www.theatlantic.com/international/archive/2015/10/europeans-comfort-touch-social-bonds/412861/

14 Juulia T. Suvilehto, Enrico Glerean, Robin I. M. Dunbar, Riitta Hari and Lauri Nummenmaa, 'Topography of Social Touching Depends on Emotional Bonds Between Humans', *PNAS*, 112:48

(1 December 2015). Available at http://www.pnas.org/content/pnas/early/2015/10/21/1519231112.full.pdf

15 Heather A. Rupp and Kim Wallen, 'Sex Differences in Response to Visual Sexual Stimuli: A Review', *Arch Sex Behav.* April 2008; 37(2): 206–18. Available at https://link.springer.com/article/10.1007/s10508-007-9217-9

16 Kate Julian, 'Why Are Young People Having So Little Sex?', *Atlantic*, December 2018. Available at https://www.theatlantic.com/magazine/archive/2018/12/the-sex-recession/573949/

17 Ibid.

18 Kari Paul, 'Pornhub Removes Millions of Videos After Investigation Finds Child Abuse Content', *Guardian*, 14 December 2020.

19 See https://forum.nofap.com/index.php?threads/no-porn-for-77-days-feeling-healthier-but-not-fixed-yet.283323/

20 See the 'NoFap' website: https://nofap.com/

21 'NoFap' forum. Available at https://forum.nofap.com/index.php

5. *Is Separatism the Answer?*

1 Paul Elam, *Men. Women. Relationships: Surviving the Plague of Modern Masculinity* (self-published, 2019), Kindle edition.

2 Ashley Parker, Twitter, 29 March 2017. Available at https://twitter.com/AshleyRParker/status/847094598136709120

3 Michel Houellebecq, *Whatever: A Novel*, trans. Paul Hammond (London: Serpent's Tail, 1998), p. 99.

4 Douglas Morrey, 'Sex and the Single Male: Houellebecq, Feminism, and Hegemonic Masculinity', *Yale French Studies*, 116–17 (2009), p. 142.

5 See https://www.reddit.com/r/TheRedPill/comments/3d8kqi/whats_a_male_smv_10/

6 Amia Srinivasan, 'Does Anyone Have the Right to Sex?', *London Review of Books* 40:6 (22 March 2018), pp. 5–10.

7 Quoted ibid.

8 Ibid.

9 See the home page at https://www.mgtow.com/

10 Kashmira Gander, 'Inside the World of Men Who've Sworn Never to Sleep with Women Again', *Independent*, 27 September 2016. Available at https://www.independent.co.uk/life-style/love-sex/reddit-mgtow-men-sex-sleep-women-manosphere-meninist-a7330276.html

11 See https://www.mgtow.com/history/

12 Friedrich Nietzsche, *On the Genealogy of Morality and Other Writings*, trans. Carol Diethe, ed. Keith Ansell-Pearson (Cambridge: Cambridge University Press, 1994), p. 81.

13 See https://www.reddit.com/r/wgtow/

14 See https://www.reddit.com/r/RedPillWomen/comments/4hmfh1/is_it_possible_for_women_to_go_their_own_way/d2r9n3y/

15 *No More Fun and Games: A Journal of Female Liberation* (1968). Available at https://library.duke.edu/digitalcollections/wlmpc_wlmms01029/

16 Richard Kreitner, 'The Stoics and the Epicureans on Friendship, Sex, and Love', *Montréal Review*, January 2012. Available at http://www.themontrealreview.com/2009/The-Stoics-and-the-Epicureans-on-Friendship-Sex-and-Love.php

17 Al Alvarez, *The Savage God: A Study of Suicide* (Harmondsworth: Penguin, 1971), p. 12.

18 Ibid., p. 48.

19 Campaign Against Living Miserably (CALM), 'Get Help On: Suicidal Thoughts'. Available at https://www.thecalmzone.net/help/get-help/suicide/

20 Office for National Statistics, *Suicides in the UK: 2017 Registrations*, 4 September 2018. Available at https://www.ons.gov.uk/peoplepopulationandcommunity/birthsdeathsandmarriages/deaths/bulletins/suicidesintheunitedkingdom/2017registrations

21 K-Punk blog, 27 July 2004. Available at http://k-punk.abstract-dynamics.org/archives/003718.html
22 See https://twitter.com/0x49fa98/status/1057382140281679873?s=20

6. *What* Do *Men Want?*

1 See Roosh's forum. Available at https://www.rooshvforum.com/archive/thread-72750.html
2 Ibid.
3 See Sigmund Freud, 'Totem and Taboo' in *The Standard Edition of the Complete Psychological Works of Sigmund Freud, Volume XIII (1913–1914): Totem and Taboo and Other Works*, ed. James Strachey (London: The Hogarth Press and the Institute of Psycho-analysis, 1955).
4 See Paul Verhaeghe, *Says Who? The Struggle for Authority in a Market-Based Society*, trans. David Shaw (London: Scribe, 2015).
5 David Cooper, *The Death of the Family* (London: Penguin Books, 1971), p. 8.
6 Alexander Mitscherlich, *Society without the Father: A Contribution to Social Psychology*, trans. Eric Mosbacher (New York: Tavistock Publications, 1969), p. 284.

Conclusion: Forgiveness and Reconciliation

1 Jean-Paul Sartre, *Dirty Hands* (New York: Vintage International, 1989), p. 189.
2 Roy F. Baumeister, *Is There Anything Good About Men? How Cultures Flourish by Exploiting Men* (Oxford: Oxford University Press, 2010), p. 6.

Index

bodies (*cont.*)
   mansplaining, 22; shame about,
   52, 77; transhumanist/futuristic
   ideas, 71, 77; and virtual world,
   52, 61
Bostrom, Nick, 71
Burke, Tarana, 23–4

Camus, Albert, *The Outsider*, 128
'cancel culture,' 3
Canetti, Elias, *Crowds and Power*,
   105–6
capitalist culture: as always
   indifferent to goodness, 50;
   debased 'equality' of, 37, 43, 49,
   89, 117, 138, 141; and dismantled
   patriarchy, 41; as encouraging
   lack of self- restraint, 134–5,
   142–3; 'freedom' offered by, 31,
   37, 138–9, 141; grand
   marketplace of "well-being,"
   92–3; and isolated, atomic
   individual, 10, 34–5, 137; as
   largely indifferent to sexual
   difference, 1–2, 49, 50, 51, 123; as
   Locke without God, 112;
   markets and sex, 117–20, 137,
   141; and mental health, 91–2,
   139–40; people as 'things,' 31,
   51, 81, 143; shift to managerial/
   bureaucratic system of control,
   37, 48–9, 115, 138–9, 142;
   short-termism, 10; totally
   surveilled modern world, 47,
   48–9, 103–5, 139; transformation
   of family structures, 82
Carlin, John, 36–7
chess, 130

children: care of, 6, 43, 44, 59, 140;
   fathers and custody issues, 74;
   reintroduction to nature, 86;
   schools in Ancient Rome, 99;
   today's lack of father figures,
   18–19, 40, 41–2, 87, 88, 133–4,
   139, 140–1, 142
Christman, Phil, 78, 79
class, 4, 27, 29, 40, 44, 47, 61,
   125, 139
Connolly, Cyril, 124
consumerism, 2, 31, 39, 41, 48, 65,
   89, 91–2, 115, 131, 132, 134–5
Cooper, David, 139–40
Cotter, David, 64–5

Daly, Mary, *Gyn/Ecology*, 39–40, 41
Deneuve, Catherine, 25, 62
desire: and abandonment of the
   sacred, 98; and amoral
   consumerism, 31, 65; clashing of
   desires, 34, 37, 72, 97, 115, 117,
   145; for economic and social
   recognition, 60–1; feminism and
   male desire, 119–20; freedom in
   controlling of, 112–14; as
   free-flowing in twentieth
   century, 145; and human
   imagination, 108; and identity,
   64, 65, 81; 'ladette' culture, 141;
   male desire to protect, 78–9;
   male residual desire for
   domination, 37; mystery,
   promise and terror of, 36, 144; in
   our selfish and immature culture,
   134–5, 142–3; for paternalistic
   figures, 18–19, 133–4, 141; and
   personal responsibility, 38, 47–8,

nature, humanity's break with, 32, 86, 138–9
Netflix, 61–2
Nietzsche, Friedrich, *The Genealogy of Morality*, 123
'NoFap' movement, 112–14

O'Malley, Harris, 24

Paglia, Camille, 50
'patriarchy,' 3, 5–6, 39–40, 119, 150; factual dimension, 40; feminist narratives of, 41, 42–3; and 'gynocentrism,' 124–5; historical reality for men, 42–3, 58; and 'male privilege' concept, 43–5; and male-on-male violence, 58; mythical dimension, 40–1; *positive* dimensions of, 41–2; society as no longer 'paternalistic,' 138–9; and use of language, 53; and virility, 62–4, 69
Pence, Mike, 116
Pepin, Joanna, 64–5
Perry, Grayson, 28, 72
Perry, Louise, 65–6
Peterson, Jordan, 18–19, 82, 133–4
'Pick-up artists' (PUAs), 18, 77, 99–103, 135–6
Planned Parenthood, 52–3
Plath, Sylvia, 126–7
Pornhub, 111
pornography, 11, 64, 108–9, 111–12; 'NoFap' movement, 112–14
'privilege' concept, 6, 27, 29, 40, 43–9

psychology, 41–2, 59, 76–7, 80–1, 82–6
Putin, Vladimir, 140–1

Raniere, Keith, 24
Real, Julian, 43–4
Recalcati, Massimo, *In Praise of Forgiveness*, 8
Reich, Wilhelm, 86
relationships: blaming and fault-finding, 9, 147; dating apps, 37, 103–4, 109, 110, 111; fantasy of the 'single other,' 9–10, 99; modern culture of sibling rivalry, 42, 137, 141, 147; need to make our own meaning, 145; ongoing hard work needed in, 9–10; and perpetual and joyful present, 146; and power imbalances, 46; 'real life' romantic encounters, 12; role of social touch in, 106–7; romantic conception of fusion, 81; 'serious,' 98–9; simplistic version of erotic love, 35; and social pressure, 97; spirit of 'graceful playfulness,' 10–11, 13, 35–6, 99, 114; survival of romantic ideal, 144–5; and totally surveilled modern world, 47, 48–9, 103–5, 139; twentieth century left's view of the couple, 10
religion, 135–6; and John Locke, 111–12; as overturned by individualism, 98–9; post-Christian age, 7–8, 98; religious texts, 35